AVAILABLE LIGHT

AVAILABLE LIGHT

HERMÉNÉGILDE CHIASSON

Translated from the French by
WAYNE GRADY

DOUGLAS & MCINTYRE
VANCOUVER/TORONTO

Douglas & McIntyre
2323 Quebec Street, Suite 201
Vancouver, British Columbia
V5T 4S7
www.douglas-mcintyre.com

NATIONAL LIBRARY OF CANADA CATALOGUING IN PUBLICATION DATA

Chiasson, Herménégilde, 1946–
[Brunante. English]
Available Light

Translation of: Brunante.

ISBN 1-55054-959-6

1. Chiasson, Herménégilde, 1946– —Anecdotes. I. Grady, Wayne. II. Title.

PS8555.H465B7813 2002   C848'.5403   C2002-910834-9
PQ3919.2.C537B7813 2002

Translation by Wayne Grady
Copy editing by Kathryn Spracklin and Saeko Usukawa
Design by Val Speidel
Printed and bound in Canada by Transcontinental
Printed on acid-free paper

The publisher gratefully acknowledges the financial support of the Canada Council
for the Arts, the British Columbia Ministry of Tourism, Small Business and Culture,
and the Government of Canada through the Book Publishing Industry Development
Program (BPIDP) for its publishing activities.

Contents

A Photographer at the Louvre

THE LOUVRE, with its glass pyramid, on a Sunday afternoon in September. It's hot. She lies back on a stone bench, her black hat straight out of the *belle époque*. With her eyes half-closed against the sun, she reminds me of a photograph by Sarah Moon. She has the same instinct for seduction. I think: in a few minutes we'll exit via the Grand Canal. I can already hear the horses in the courtyard, see the musketeers with their plumes, the entire scene dredged up from a childhood spent in front of a TV set watching Jean Marais leap onto his horse from a second-storey balcony in I-don't-remember-which film. She leaves.

She is taking photographs in the Louvre's shadowy galleries. None of them will turn out. I could tell her that, but then I know she'd take three times as many just to show me that it's none of my business. So I say nothing, remain in the background, watching the coach-and-four gather speed along the rue de Rivoli. The king is fleeing the city.

It's very hot. All winter the people have been emptying their chamber pots into the canal, and now that the sun is heating up the whole mess, the stench is unbearable. Which is why the king is fleeing. No, it's not the Revolution yet; he has simply decided to go hunting. To get away from the stink. To Fontainebleau, or Versailles, or Chambord. She doesn't care, she has more important things to do. Such as taking these badly lit photographs. What an age we live in.

With all these scenes, these permutations of superstition and the history of art spinning around in my head at the speed of thought, I find myself standing before David's immense painting, *The Coronation of Josephine*. Bonaparte's mother, dressed entirely in black, is staring me right in the eye. She always referred to her daughter-in-law as "the whore." Bonaparte himself is holding aloft the crown, a symbol of the vanity that will eventually destroy him. At least that's how we always explained his memorable defeat in our family. "God gives this to me, and God help whoever takes it away," he is supposed to have said as he took the crown from the hands of the pope, whom he had summoned to Paris for the occasion, and placed it on Josephine's head. There is something laughable, something kitschy, in the way the burghers are just standing there: their overblown splendour, their silk stockings, holding their ostrich-feathered hats in their hands. Is this how they chose to have themselves immortalized?

For technique, I still prefer Ingres, David's contemporary, even though he did add a few vertebrae to give his *Odalisque* more height. Here she is, larger than life, so different from the miniature colour reproduction of her in the dictionary that we furtively passed around from desk to desk, no doubt in anticipation of *Playboy* centrefolds. All she lacked were two staples in her ass, a sado-masochistic detail that Duchamp would not have resisted adding. I look at the painting, its smooth pictorial line, nothing in it to betray its artful execution, no brush stroke, no momentary hesitation, only that disconcerting technical virtuosity. I remember the petition Ingres signed, protesting the recognition of photography as one of the fine arts. Perhaps he felt photography was too close to his own work?

She takes another photo. I could tell her that the varnish will act as a mirror when her flash hits it, that when she develops the print, all she'll get is the slave-woman's face with an immense white cloud in the centre of the print. And so Ingres will be both vindicated and punished.

In the Renaissance room with its undeniable masterpieces, especially the *Mona*, smiling enigmatically behind her Plexiglas screen. Here, too, flashbulbs cause much subsequent disappointment, the varnish cloud replaced by its modern equivalent, the glare of plastic, put there to protect *La Giaconda* from the hired assassins who have been on her trail ever since she left the Chateau Amboise, where she slept with Leonardo. She later betrayed him with Louis XIV, and later still with Napoleon; both of them kept her locked up in their bedrooms. But in this room she takes no photographs. Instead, she watches the circus, the jostling crowd, impatient for our moment of truth in the lineup, the ultimate verification that we can worship a masterpiece and still hold our own against the weight of the past. The more we live the more we see, and we await the fateful moment when our eyes will be opened forever.

Unnoticed, eclipsed in the blinding glare of the masterpiece of masterpieces, tilted slightly to the left, is Titian's *Man with Glove*, whose expression is a thousand times more interesting than that of the lady beside him. The difference between his look and her smile is the difference between a window on the soul and a painted come-on. The man stands holding his glove in his black canvas as though in mourning, except for a few exquisite hints emerging from the darkness like thoughts, like the contemplation of destiny, or the conflicting demands of a storm-laden sky whose distant thunder we cannot quite hear.

Meanwhile, in another room, there is always *The Seated Scribe*, his eyes staring for centuries at the point at which all lines of perspective meet and cancel each other out, where his gaze folds into her gaze as she ensures their survival on her split-second field of thin celluloid. Has she brought enough film to freeze the dreams of an entire age?

The Unbearable Lightness

O NE DECEMBER night in 1990, I remember watching, on French television, a famous soccer player, it might have been Michel Platini, regaling viewers with his recollections of the decade that had just ended. He was one of a panel of celebrities, all of whom were asked to liven up the show by beginning each sentence with "I remember . . . ," a bit like in the book by Perec that has that phrase for the title. Platini, let's say it was him, dredged up a few random memories, then suddenly declared: "I remember reading *The Unbearable Lightness of Being*, by Milan Kundera." Thunderstruck, I found myself wondering what would happen if, say, Mario Lemieux were being interviewed on the CBC after a hockey game and suddenly blurted out, "I remember reading *L'Homme rapaillé*, by Gaston Miron."

Someone once lent me his mother's copy of Kundera's book. This was before I'd been informed, one morning in France, that Kundera was the greatest novelist in the world. That pronouncement came from Philippe Sollers over a crackling clock radio I was using as an alarm clock in a sunny room I shared with M. in the Canadian student residence. At the time I had undertaken to read all of Kundera. I loved the fact that he was never content to amuse his readers with clever little charades but focussed, instead, on the writing itself, a modernist strategy that places the emphasis on the material, with the subject as pretext and the artist as bearer of the argument.

The book had a black cover with nothing on it but the title, as though nothing should contaminate the real encounter, which was that of words with other words, a strangely symbiotic relationship brought about by the juxtaposition of letters, even though everyone agrees that the alphabet is nothing but a tool. I read it in an airport, completely oblivious to the noise, the press of human bodies, the normal laws of fluid and thermal dynamics, deaf to everything but Kundera's words. I kept asking myself where on Earth had such understanding had come from. At a conference I attended somewhere, Duane Michaels, in the staccato delivery style that is his trademark, said that great artists are in a certain sense gifts that come to us at moments when we absolutely least expect them. Kundera is such a gift, as are Pina Bausch, Bob Wilson, Robert Frank, Jasper Johns, Cy Twombly, Antoni Tàpies, Josef Beuys, Wim Wenders and Martin Scorsese. We always wonder where they come from, of what solitude they are the unforeseen, the unhoped-for, manifestations.

The film came out in 1988, another of those made from a book as unfilmable as a work of Proust. They would have had to resort to some kind of internal voice-over, as in Duras, to achieve the same interiority as the novel. Instead, they settled for the storyline, which is as banal as any other, despite the disturbing expression on Juliette Binoche's face and the evocation of that spring in Prague with archival footage that occasionally lends the film the authenticity of documentary. Why do we persist in turning books into films when we so rarely do the opposite? Could film ever be anything to Kundera other than a vehicle for popularity, an aura of lightness that renders tolerable everything that disappears into the folds of our memory? Perhaps I'm underestimating the desires film generates and suggests, the number of people who would sell their souls to see their names scrolling up there on the big screen in the luminous letters of the credits that no one ever reads.

Cinema is the art of rupture, of splintering, of fragmentation. No wonder our thoughts come to us in their most fractured form when they are relayed via television, or video, or the Internet, or what have you. Modernity, our modern world, is a place of innumerable ruptures. Kundera understood that; it is what he reproduced in his complex and breathtaking ellipses, which remind me most of the work of Robert Rauschenberg: tonality instead of colour, the whole balanced in a delicate montage, an erudite equilibrium of the intuited and the known.

I am rereading *Pas pire*, by the Acadian writer France Daigle, and wondering if Kundera isn't Acadian himself. That would explain why his work hits me so hard. His way of understating everything, of letting there be long silences, of always holding something back, the slowness reflected in the title of his book. There is this impossible plurality that we reproduce in our books, combined with a lack of conviction that slows us down, freezes us in our tracks. Such persecuted prose condemns us, too, to silence, but what is there in silence? All the sadness of the world, yes, of course, but also a host of other absences, resonances, echoes, pain.

So someone lent me his mother's copy of *The Unbearable Lightness of Being*. I still have it, with its black dust jacket. I never returned it. I must have forgotten, but what is it about forgetfulness that we allow it to become permanent? It's a first edition. His mother has since died. He and I have lost touch. Not because of the book, no, that would have been too stupid, but because we were caught up in a kind of dance that allowed us to perceive each other's obvious faults at the beginning of the relationship and gradually ignore them, so that in the end they became so enormous that we couldn't see anything else. The pain of rejection. We got back together, briefly, but on ground still undermined by our dormant faults. We'd catch glimpses of them from time to time if we looked hard enough, the hand on the coverlet, too smooth and still glistening with this unforgettable book. Obvious ruptures that we forget about until they fly at us from a bookshelf, our eyes having fallen on the spine of a favourite book, left behind by someone who thinks it lost.

The Discovery of Necessity

MY BROTHER taught school in Saint-Simon, a village of one thousand people in northwestern New Brunswick. This was in pre–Louis Robichaud days. Robichaud was the premier whose reforms led to the Acadian version of Quebec's Quiet Revolution. Schools in my day were funded by means of a special tax, a system that ensured that students from wealthy parts of the province were taught under better conditions than those that prevailed in, for example, Saint-Simon. Our teachers often had to wait for their paycheques because the taxes providing their salaries were returned somewhat irregularly.

My brother told me that one day, as a special treat, he would take me to school with him. He taught in a small, white school house. There were two classrooms, both heated with wood in winter. The toilets were outside. There was no running water. In one of the rooms sat students from grades one to three; in the other, my brother was the only teacher, and he had to cover all the subjects for grades four through eight. He told me I could spend a whole day in the grade one classroom.

At the time, there were no paved roads, and in winter it was often difficult to travel. Snow tended to be allowed to pile up. Sometimes, if it was necessary to get a pregnant woman or someone who was sick to a hospital, they would get out the snow blower instead of the plows, which were always breaking down on those rough roads. Otherwise, we would just wait for the snow to melt.

When the promised day arrived, I took my place at one of the wooden desks in the junior room, aware of the fact that I was an object of curiosity for the other students. The teacher, a pleasant woman whose voice I remember as calming, took my new scribbler and, at the top of one of the pages, wrote a series of letters that I was supposed to copy on the lines below.

I found the work fastidious, disconcerting and boring. I

quickly lost interest. Instead of applying myself to this stupefy-
ing task, I decided to expend my energies by drawing a Royal
Canadian Mounted Police officer. I had taught myself to draw
a fairly realistic Mountie hat; drawing the hat was, in fact, the
main source of pleasure I took in drawing the man. Everything
but the hat was relegated to the level of detail and pretext.
Drawing and redrawing the hat, tracing its elliptical form and
then inserting a head in it like an egg in an egg cup, filled me
with a joy that must have been like that felt by Alberti when he
first happened upon the laws of perspective. I had leapt a major
hurdle in the path of my self-imposed artistic apprenticeship,
and I thought I would share the moment with the teacher who,
being busy, had left me for the day to the traditional, repetitive
labours generally associated with the acquisition of the rudi-
ments of alphabetical codification, imagining that I was taking
pleasure in the work that she had so distractedly assigned to me.

I remember that she had spent a good deal of time drawing,
with a ruler, a series of pencil lines exactly between the blue lines
already printed on the pages of my new scribbler, so that the
descenders and the ascenders of the letters would be contained
within their own rigid structures. My drawing covered many of

her lines, creating a sort of palimpsest, or allegory, of disfiguration, obscuring the great system devised for the transmission of all Western thought. No doubt about it, I had committed an act of terrorism, probably Freudian at its base.

My poor, innocent figure in graphite—or silverpoint, as it was called in the Renaissance—defied the most elementary rules of aesthetics. I obviously cared for nothing but the obsessive repetition of a single, emblematic form. I had taken a Platonic approach, creating a work that was limited entirely to imitation. My choice of subject matter was not important to me; all that mattered was the performance, in the Chomskian sense of the term. Do better the next time, do what is possible now.

When she came to look over my work at the end of the morning session, I showed her my drawing, tingling with certainty that she would be greatly impressed by such an accomplishment. Imagine my disappointment when I saw her face cloud as she realized that she had been deceived, a realization that was quickly translated into reprobation for my refusal to conform to the prescribed exercise.

At home, my mother would go into raptures at my slightest dabblings, but here at school I was encountering someone who demanded I conform to her code and learn her signs in order to earn her affection, or at the least her approval. There was something in her attitude that frightened me: perhaps an intimation that the world would turn out to be nothing more than this constraining and derisory thing whose relevance I would have to evaluate very quickly. I do know that from that day on, I retreated into my own thoughts, constantly reformulating a strategy that would allow me to follow and improve on the rigorous work I had accomplished up to that time. If I didn't, I would run the risk of being carried away by other currents of ideas, other systems of thought, which I was afraid would defeat me.

Since that day, I have been persuaded that being an artist has nothing to do with pleasing someone; its value is measured entirely by the outward expression of an internal rigour that is independent of success, satisfaction or fame.

First Exhibition

A ROOM in a library basement. The time isn't right, or maybe it's the place. Everything is jumbled together. Each of us is intensely aware that Modern Times are about to arrive any day now, and we are scrambling to make room for them, but we don't quite know what the long-term consequences are going to be. We work up impressions, we tinker, we start something and give it up, we experiment with new material or the immaterial or the ephemeral, we do action paintings. We've all seen Pollock, and he makes us feel left behind, and we don't really know what else there is to look at. News comes to us so late here, and there is no one to explain it to us. So we wait, killing time by practising the art of imitation.

There is, no doubt about it, a desire for a new dimension. Some may see this as an insurmountable contradiction in terms, this need to fall in with the modern world without losing our own self-awareness, our own individuality. We do not know that the strategy we should adopt is that of reference: inserting little vectors in our work so that the reader or viewer will know where we're coming from. (Obviously, we had to code these vectors so that they carried the maximum information and importance: footnotes at the bottom of the page, for example, like Réjean Ducharme in *L'Hiver de force*. In the meantime, we were still doing mimetic art.)

Modernism as a generic term was a cover for our contemporary existence. We wanted to show ourselves to our best advantage, to put our best new ideas forward. Those from the outside questioned us, told us that it all looked like the research part of a thesis, that it was dangerous for us to play at being the sorcerer's apprentices. Acadians were supposed to be happy in their exoticism. The costume looked so good on us, and we had this singsong accent; why would we want to give it all up for a sudden, fatal loss of naïveté?

The age-old chant arose, powerful in its purpose, overwhelming in its tone, telling us not to abandon the deportees of yesteryear, that our survival had been a miracle and that we had to present ourselves in ways laid down for us by those who imagined us in our own image and our own likeness. Our modest efforts at modernity would be swept away like so many castles in the sand; we would watch the current carry off the frail barque of our dreams, all our words lost at sea.

My Last Painting

THE STUDIO was completely glassed-in except at eye level, so that the models could not be seen from outside during life-drawing classes. Sometime during the last night I spent in it, in 1972, I was unaccountably seized by the need to give up painting forever. Then my senses became aware of something mixed in with the smell of linseed oil from the workshops: her thin body, her eyes, her loneliness as she came in wrapped in a black sheet.

I had one canvas left. I decided to soak it in the entire contents of a can of black paint, industrial strength. The cloth was soon so completely saturated that black liquid floated on the surface of it like an oil slick. It was the age of minimalist art:

aesthetic considerations dictated that you had to dye the canvas, a subtlety that no doubt caused more ink to flow than paint and bewildered everyone.

It was late at night and I was tired. In my mind, her black sheet bled away into an infinity of snow; she was a cameo from another era, a dark figure on a platform in some obscure railway station. Lost in concentration, she moved with her arms crossed over her breasts, as though the linoleum floor were a field of ice and she were stepping into a universe in which painting no longer mattered. The air around her reeked of turpentine.

Daylight seeped into the sky, but my canvas remained as black as ever, an oily swamp holding the reflection of stars, a mirror of heaven. In a fit of despair and complacency, my eyes fell on an aerosol spray can, and, seizing it, I sprayed a silver border around the solid black mass. Then I threw myself down on the mattress that was there to ease the long poses of tired models.

I dreamed. I was floating on an infinite surface, black and turbulent. A sort of premonition. In the distance, where my own life was to take place later, I heard the sounds of an exhibition; the prime minister was there, and lots of other people. I was with her. I had had too much to drink. I still loved her. Why did I love her? What did she have that I loved? Was it her refusal, her distance, her chilliness? She worked in communications.

When she died, no one mentioned the sadness that had so completely possessed her. In what dark corner of her life had she encountered the virus that would eventually consume her? In a drawing for which she had posed, you saw her lifting her arms to the sky. She might have been a Giacometti figure; she had that exalted tension, her silhouette in a state of weightlessness.

As for me, I'm still here, still pondering the meaning of beauty, wondering why life always gets its way.

Angels from Dupuis Frères

I T HELPS if you understand that the pages of the Dupuis Frères catalogue were a kind of dreamscape. True, the features in the English magazines were more luxurious, more seductive, but it was Dupuis Frères, with its dark pages and enigmatic descriptions, the wondrousness of its products, hitting us just as we were entering the stage of prepubescent ritual and initiation, that fed our French-Canadian, Catholic fervour. All the more so as we were old enough to imagine the objects whose glossy images so intrigued us.

I was seven years old in 1953, the year of the Marian Congress, when everyone paraded from church to church behind a statue of the Madonna on a flatbed trailer that was made to haul bulldozers. Each visitation lasted three days and was followed by knock-down, drag-out sessions of hysterical praying, a sort of religious blitzkrieg, with invocations to the Blessed Virgin to halt the relentless advance of Communism throughout the free world.

At school we had to keep a Mary Notebook, a special scribbler that we filled with collages made from bits of holy images, clippings of cherubs with their heads sprouting from pairs of fluffy wings, and those pastel metallic paper stars that were sprinkled randomly among the people chanting for world peace. Obviously, I had to take part in this demonstration of mass hysteria. My contribution, late but no less intense for that, was made with the assistance of my brother acting as my art director.

It must have been the package that arrived from Dupuis Frères that fired my imagination. It contained the store's entire selection of religious images, one hundred of them, no two alike, and sheet upon sheet of angels on gummed paper. They were for our scholarly montages. I'm pretty sure now that my fascination had more to do with the rapturous faces of the angels, which dazzled me with their profusion of acid colours, than with any role they might have played as spiritual envoys or guides from Above.

But I see my father, illiterate, silent, lying in bed throughout those long winter days, flipping through catalogues to fool himself into believing he wasn't confined to a world of incessant wind, and being transported to one in which his misery was redeemed by these flimsy instruments of escape. He probably preferred the English catalogues with their full-colour illustrations, their offers of a Third World rendered beautiful and proud by the colourful, vibrating shimmer of its tribal dances. His, I think, was a more complicated, a more costly, illusion.

Évangéline

MY MOTHER and I had come to an agreement. She would buy me a complete set of tubes of oil paint on condition that I would make her a copy of a portrait of Évangéline that showed her looking out over the shore where the Acadians had been forced onto the English ships when they were deported from their land. The original of this portrait had been painted by my brother ages ago, but it had been lost. And the cover of the book that had been the portrait's model, *The Touching Odyssey of Évangéline*, by Eugène Achard, had likewise disappeared from the family archives. I was, therefore, charged to reproduce it from memory, to dive into the murky depths of my brain to come up with whatever pearls

I could find to reference my future masterpiece. I had become, although I didn't know it at the time, a bit like Géricault, who, in order to paint *The Raft of the "Medusa,"* shaved off half his hair so that he wouldn't be tempted to leave his studio until the painting was completed. The fateful package arrived and I set to work, painting non-stop on a large piece of cardboard, actually the back of a Pepsi-Cola poster that a distributor had left in my mother's general store.

The figure was barely sketched in when I decided to plow straight ahead to the end. Not wanting to use up all my little tubes on this one painting, I decided to do the bulk of it in house paint. We had some blue and white oil-based enamel that I thought would do for the sky, which, in a landscape, always took up a huge percentage of the surface area. The problem, as I discovered as soon as the paint had dried, was in the deadly flat uniformity of the blue, which made the thing look more like a wall than the cloud-tormented sky I had had in mind. I decided to use my tube of white to touch it up a bit around the edges with a few clouds, but since the undercoat was the kind of paint that also acts as a sealant, the oil didn't have a ghost of a chance of being properly absorbed, and I had to resign myself to having two competing techniques jammed together on a single work, thus anticipating the postmodernist vision long before its artistic time had come.

In any case, I consoled myself with the execution of what I believed to be an uncommonly complicated effect in the form of a tree, a species of weeping willow whose drooping branches seemed to me to prefigure the inconsolable tears that would soon be flowing down my heroine's cheeks as, in the foreground, she endeavoured to convey to the viewer the immeasurable depths of sorrow to which fate had condemned her. But first I was to come up against the second major obstacle in my quest to wring my material of its secrets; this came when I attempted to mix yellow and blue directly on the work itself in order to produce a green in which the hairs of my brush would leave a pattern of tiny traces suggesting the sort of filigreed effect I somehow associated with grass. This may, in fact, have been my one true discovery about painting: that it functions as a system capable of producing effects and reactions no other medium can claim, a system to which very few people these days pay much attention except to relive the joys of yesteryear. Velázquez is dead, and Renoir has orphaned us, leaving us his palette of pixels, which we use to make our CD-ROMs more appealing. No doubt someone someday will write the same thing when the secrets of digitalization have disappeared into the vast abysses of time, writing itself having given way to the raised voice.

The work progressed slowly. At one point during the summer, just as the painting was nearing completion, my brother came by and made some disparaging comment, the details of which I can no longer call to mind but the effect of which was to launch me into a fit of blind rage. I mashed what was left of my paints onto the piece of cardboard I was using as a palette and smeared them across much of the painting. My mother, alerted to the disaster, descended onto the field of battle and negotiated yet another peace treaty. After reprimanding my brother, she tried to calm me down by telling me that he probably hadn't fully appreciated the effect his criticism would have on someone of my creative sensibilities and that he was moreover a compromised critic because it was he who had painted the original version of the work of which I was trying to make a copy.

Criticism, no matter how harsh, always bows out when the

mind is engaged in the sheer persistence of the work. I decided to put that principle into operation and finish the painting. When it was done, I inscribed my name and the year at the bottom, on the black frame that I had painted around the whole thing.

My brother's comment is long forgotten, but I still have the painting. I look at it from time to time to help bring back that moment of innocent ecstasy when painting opened itself up to me like a cupboard full of magic spells.

When I look at the sad figure of Évangéline I see a drawing floating on a base of deep pink enamel. Since that time, I've learned how easy it is to become lost in that pictorial paste, although drawing helps to keep our heads on straight. Had I been more willing to explore Évangéline's pain, to dive into its crests and troughs, I'm sure I would have produced a more affecting work than these brush strokes floating forever on the too-smooth surface of paint.

But it was summer, it was hot, the days were endless, and I knew nothing about anything. I was into my adolescence . . . soon I would be into Blaise Cendrars, or maybe Rimbaud. Rimbaud, yes. Certainly, soon I would be into Rimbaud.

Pray for Him

PARIS WRAPPED us in its silken cocoon and its mystery. Escape, novelty, discovery—in short, adventure—was our only driving force, although we did have a car. A good car, more or less, and the Verlaine-Rimbaud route was clearly marked by signs depicting the figures of the two poets. We sailed down the foggy roads in search of the myth that had inspired the birth of the modern.

Between Paris and Charleville-Mézières (a town which, like Québec, was founded in 1608), we stopped in Reims, champagne country, knowing he wouldn't have minded such a diversion. There was the cathedral: I couldn't help thinking that his eyes must also have rested on this edifice, which, despite its reputation as a work of art, failed to convince me that it wasn't first and foremost a church and that the nature of his relationship with Verlaine had, in his own words, caused the wounds in the side of Our Lord Jesus Christ miraculously to bleed again.

Back on the road. Just before sunset, we arrived at the station. It was in a park in which people were warned to keep their dogs on leashes and which contained a statue that looked nothing at all like him. There were also notices announcing a series of rock concerts. We checked into the Modern Hotel, and, a bit later, feeling famished, we wandered with Claude and Marcia into the bright, humid, foggy town in search of a restaurant. Perhaps prey to the kind of hallucinations that beset many travellers who stray too long in the desert, we began to notice that all the young men in the town looked like him. A trick of the light, a profound emanation or a banal projection of our own subconscious—who could say? But we were convinced that he was appearing to us, insinuating himself into their bodies in search of a final, if somewhat unsettled, resting place.

Graffiti coated the stone walls and the tall arcade that bordered the central square, spray paint over stencils, a technique that made it possible to produce a lot of images in a short time.

They formed a kind of repetitive pattern, discreet and even sophisticated compared to the aggressively eloquent examples found in America, where graffiti is a form of protest against the anonymity of the megacity, especially New York.

The next day, after visiting the museum and watching the Meuse lying langorously in its narrow bed, and having provisioned ourselves with little chocolate figurines of him and photographed everything we could think of that would prove we had been there, we headed towards the cemetery, a place of high expectations and the ultimate goal of our odyssey.

A light rain had begun to fall, a steady drizzle that coated the grey headstones and iron crosses with a glistening patina, their hieratic silhouettes thrusting graffiti-laden arms towards a lofty, inquisitorial heaven. We were looking for the spot where all his rebelliousness had been reabsorbed. And there he was, under a tiny square of earth on which someone had placed a small stone structure surmounted by a black metal cross on which we read this curious message: "Pray for Him."

There came to my mind a memory, more like a suite of thoughts and anecdotes, concerning the fate of those writers among us who come from families that are insensitive and even hostile to the complicated and unpredictable demands that writing makes. Pray for us. I thought of his mother, her son a poet at the age of seven. Of his sister Isabelle who, with her husband Paterne Berrichon, doctored his manuscripts after his death, a betrayal not unlike that of Nietzsche's sister who changed her brother's papers to make them more compatible with the ideologies of the Third Reich. Pray for them.

Rimbaud the rebel, forerunner of Kerouac, he of the monumental, unforgettable pub crawls, vengeful and insulting in the bars of Lowell, Massachussets, having returned exhausted and disillusioned from staying too long on the road, seeking a truer deliverance in alcohol. I thought of Kerouac's grave, dug deep into the American soil, a plain slab of granite set in the anonymous grass. You can sit on that slab, have a drink, have a whole party, a ritual ridding of the body of dust from the Industrial Revolution or of nuclear fallout from the fear of the bomb. They leave him gifts, anything to make the dead feel at home: poems, drugs, booze, condoms, cassettes. A body shouldn't be lonely. Tributes to the words he left behind, themselves following their own voyage of initiation, engendering other words, constantly renewing themselves in an attempt to affirm the body's continued twitching despite the fact that the mortician's recommended procedures have been meticulously followed.

"It was the myth of the rainy night," he wrote, proclaiming, as have so many others, his kinship with Rimbaud. Solitude in the din of machinery, liberation when they shut it down and you can move on to the Moulin de la Galette or have a drink in the Bar des Folies-Bergères. Rimbaud nimbused in the halo of his own genius, possessor of a gift he couldn't ignore: a talent like da Vinci's for seeing beauty in spit, a unique way of talking that slakes the body's immense thirst for language.

Picasso: Slips of the Pen, Lapses of Memory

I T IS SAID *that during his Pink Period, Picasso would often go to the Medrano Circus to watch the clowns and acrobats, convinced that their performances perfectly mirrored the* artist's frame of mind.

Which makes me wonder if I, too, need, have a right to—not just need but absolutely deserve—a Medrano Circus of my own.

He would have seen Toulouse-Lautrec's acrobats, and Seurat's, and Degas's horses and dancers and nudes. Renoir's failed attempts to recreate Rubens's flesh tones. On Sundays, the races on the Grande Jatte. That famous poster of Lautrec's, the one with La Goulue strolling into the Moulin Rouge on the arm of Valentin the Contortionist. Later, in an asylum, at death's door, weighing little more than an old rag doll, she would tell her confessor over and over again: "I am La Goulue. I am La Goulue."

He would have known the world of prostitutes, of endless afternoons wasted in Manet's blue-green cafés; Manet, whose hand Cézanne refused to shake because, he said, it was dirtied. In one of his acrobat paintings, there is a monkey so human-looking it appears to be eating at the same table with them. At the end of his life, he pictured himself as an aged monkey, painting diaphanously clad women whose skin was even more satiny than the women in Goya's *Maja Desnuda*. The old acrobat looking on as his child does backflips on a ball. His body had become a monument.

Pink; the colour of asylums, the universal sedative.

Picasso knew all this.

But before the Medrano Circus, he had to undergo a blue period, his Blue Period.

In the winter of 1973, I remember staggering with exhaustion, driving down to Louisiana in an old van with three friends. We drove day and night. After two days we were in the melodious bayous, contemplating their gloomy atmosphere. On a beach in Florida, I had read a collection of articles on conceptual art and *It's Your Turn, Laura Cadieux*, laughing out loud. In an old issue of *Rolling Stone*, I read that the most important influence on the '70s music scene would be Lou Reed.

In New York, on the way back, we went into the Museum of Modern Art where, at the top of a staircase, we saw the famous, the monumental, that cold-as-ice aberration, *Guernica*. A scream in Prussian blue, shouted at Franco, at planes that dropped shrapnel bombs, against mangled, dismembered corpses. A cruel world denounced on a cruel canvas, pure vitriol, words we use only when we realize that horror has no name. And, of course, there is the anecdote: the Gestapo entering his studio, seeing the canvas, asking, "Did you do that?" and his reply, "No, you did." The cold fury. The painting not shown in Spain until after the death of Franco. There is some obscurity. When it was reproduced in a special issue of *Life* magazine dedicated to

Picasso, an unimpressed reader wrote, "I've always thought of *Guernica* as my favourite cartoon."

Someone has said that, during his Blue Period, Picasso and his friend Max Jacob owned only one pair of shoes between them, that when one went out, the other had to stay home.

(Excerpt from an interview-in-progress:)

"Prussian blue is the least expensive oil colour. They say that was why Picasso chose it during the years now known as his Blue Period. It has a cool tint, quite different from the majesty of ultramarine or the sumptuous elegance of cobalt. I think too much has been made of the hardship of those years. It has been said, for example, that Picasso and Max Jacob, with whom he shared a studio, possessed only a single pair of shoes, and that they shared the shoes when they went out. Obviously, such a story perpetuates the myth that the artist must be miserably poor, an outcast, if he is to produce anything of consequence . . ."

"Are you saying that we have invented Picasso?"

"I wouldn't go so far as to say that, but I do believe that fame accommodates itself to two significant factors: longevity and malleability. The worldly artist of the nineteenth century gave way in the twentieth to the artist in revolt against the world, the anguished martyr to art. The appeal is obvious. I don't know how much you know about the stupendous fortune Picasso had when he died, but I'm sure we can agree that he was, shall we say, comfortably off . . ." (laughs)

"Yes, but it was others who benefited from it. And the Blue Period, the Bateau-Lavoir, frostbite in the attic, surely you can't deny that these were real deterrents. That he lived . . . solely for his art . . ."

It should be noted, in passing, that Picasso was the director of the Prado, the largest museum in Spain, until his voluntary exile from that country, an exile from which he never returned.

Madrid. The Prado. The painter looks pensively at the painting of the little princess in her blue organdy dress, surrounded by dwarves. *Las Meninas.* The work hangs alone in a room swarming with tourists. At the far end, a mirror, the purpose of which is difficult to understand. Velázquez, Goya and, above all, El Greco, *The Burial of Count Orgaz.* Picasso has them all before him.

***

Barcelona. The Picasso Museum. Down a quiet, shaded street, Picasso finally has his mausoleum. A few youthful sketches of his father, roughs of the *Guernica*, a series of variations on themes from Delacroix (*Women of Algiers*) and Velázquez (*Las Meninas*). Velázquez is in very good light. Using six-foot brushes, he would have preferred to paint princesses, all the while waiting for Renoir and the Impressionists to come along to distend him into fragmentation. Janson says that Velázquez, unlike Rembrandt, was obsessed with the optical qualities of light and not merely with its metaphysical properties.

Montreal. The Museum of Fine Arts. Nicole Blondin. Someone once asked why Frank Stella's paintings are so uncompromisingly minimalist. "Because," she says, "he goes to the Met, sees Velázquez, knows there is no point redoing Velázquez, goes back to his studio and paints strips of colour."

Jean-Luc Godard's *Pierrot le fou*. Remember the beautiful scene in which Belmondo reads a phrase from Élie Faure to his child? "'At the end of his life, Velázquez painted only light.' Listen, child, listen . . ."

He would spend weeks deciding whether or not to go to a bullfight.

Françoise Gilot, in her book *Life with Picasso*, writes that he always complained that no one would take him to a bullfight, that he was surrounded by people who wanted to keep him isolated from life. And so everyone made a big fuss about trying to get him to a bullfight. At first he would agree, then almost always change his mind at the last minute.

There are, of course, a number of allusions to bullfighting in Picasso's work. The *duende*, the afternoon when death carves its pernicious shadow in the sand, in blood. Homage to the beast, to its courage, to its convulsive strength. The Spanish fascination with the spectacle of death. Hemingway's, too, for that matter. *For Whom the Bell Tolls* and *Death in the Afternoon*.

I once saw a very beautiful photograph of Picasso taken during a bullrun held in his honour. It had so many flowers and colours that, if you didn't know it was a photograph, you'd think it was a holy image. Pablo Picasso floating in the sky.

Gilot tells us how hard it was to tell him that you loved him. He always believed that he was loved for his painting, never for himself.

His exile was easy on him. It provided an excuse for his subsidized hell.

Picasso refused to return to Spain while Franco was in power. His was thus a defining exile, like Joyce's, whose reconstruction of Dublin in *Ulysses* has been said to be more real than the city itself. You can take a guided tour of "Joyce's Dublin." He recalled each street with such precision, each smell, every colour, every texture of light and shadow carved by the sun from the sky, as he toiled to create his memorable moments.

1984, in a pub in Dublin called the Molly Bloom. I hadn't known that Molly Bloom existed anywhere but in the book, but there she was, on the wall, a huge, blown-up photograph of her, with a text describing her real life, as well as various artifacts that had once belonged to her. It was a Saturday night, and the Irish were hard-drinking their celebrated magic potion. Through the window, I watched the sun going down, spreading its golden light on the Liffey, and a line of Joyce's jumped into my head, one that he wrote to his daughter when her mind was as troubled as the surface of this river, when she floated on it like Ophelia. "Why do you always sit at the window?" he asked her, looking up at the burnished Irish sky. "No doubt it makes a pretty picture, but a girl in a field also makes a pretty picture."

All exiles should be like that. They must have the courage to leave a place and say forever: after this, everything is a trance. To know that the only permanence you will ever feel will be in movement. A rough destiny, like that of animals, the heart heaving with memory. To get up each morning to face the same canvas, the familiar rage. To reproduce on canvas or paper the sound of light, the colour of voice, the texture of face, the known background, the ungraspable odour of the sea. To be in perpetual transformation, unendingly seduced; the flood of reproaches for our not being there.

There is a wonderful photograph of Picasso on the beach at Golfe-Juan, holding an immense parasol over the head of his mistress, Françoise Gilot. A very relaxed, carefree afternoon. One can see the wind playing in the fabric of Françoise's dress, pressing it against her legs. She is turned around and smiling, as though surprised by a bit of playful violence. Farther on, behind Picasso, is his nephew, Javier Vilato. One wonders what he's doing in the photograph. The parasol extends to the top of the photograph, the handle a straight

line down the middle. Françoise looms very large in the foreground,
Picasso a bit less so, and Vilato very small behind. One could well
ask why . . . etc.

No real need to give all their names, since those who know their art history are already familiar enough with them. But for the uninitiated, here they are, along with their areas of expertise. Fernande Olivier: the Pink and Blue Periods. For Cubism, Marcelle Humbert, whom Picasso called Eva. Olga Khokhlova, who was with the Russian ballet: the Classical Period. Marie-Thérèse Walter: the Graphic Period, which wove through the 1930s. Dora Maar for the horrors of the Second World War. Françoise Gilot for the high spirits of the post-war period. Jacqueline Roque for the time leading up to his death—she committed suicide shortly afterwards. Add to the list his numerous flings and the whores he hung out with in his youth. Although he knew a great number of women, there is no reason to suppose that he strove to emulate the figure given out by the novelist Georges Simenon, who boasted of having had ten thousand women, eight thousand of them prostitutes.

After the Second World War, Picasso became a veritable

cult figure, the epitome of modern art. Certain photographers, such as Robert Capa and David Douglas Duncan, were admitted into his entourage. They took photographs of him in the most unusual poses, which only increased his already enormous reputation. As part of his inner circle, they photographed him at the beach, in his studio, and entertaining the many celebrities who showed up at California, which was a rather Hollywoodish name for the residence of an artist at the peak of his fame. Robert Capa was known for his photograph of a Spanish soldier taken at the moment he was killed by a bullet, his rifle falling from his hands, his eyes squeezed shut against the pain, a testimony to the immense drama of death. It was a photograph Picasso must surely have seen. Capa himself had been under fire while photographing the Normandy invasion. All his negatives but eleven were destroyed by a careless lab technician, who left them too long in the dryer. Capa died in the field of battle in 1954, when he stepped on an anti-personel mine while covering the war in Indochina.

The parasol is the major focal element of the photo, placed as it is in the centre, its handle extending from the bottom of the frame to the top. Picasso is wearing a flowered shirt half unbuttoned. There are a number of photos of him during this period, in which he paints almost naked, his thickset torso, his hairless bearing, engaged in a sort of hand-to-hand combat with the canvas. His famous eyes, the eyes of a predator. Or of an artist. The eyes are the very essence of his myth. Dali had the same eyes, the same bulging glare (a little more commercialized, perhaps), which he probably took from Picasso, whom he worshipped in a way that was almost Oedipal, as he himself admitted. Picasso was not unaware of the effect of his eyes on others, and even made a blow-up of his face, on which he superimposed a drawing of an owl.

Having memorized this photograph, I thought of it when I read what Françoise wrote when she and Picasso were separated. He appeared to her one night, she says, sat down on the side of their bed and talked about little bits of paper, in an almost total state of distraction.

He had two children with Françoise: Claude and Paloma. At the time she became his mistress, she was twenty-one and he was sixty-two. She had gone into a café with Alan Cluny, and when Picasso saw her he went up and presented her with a bowl of cherries, a rare gift indeed during the Second World War.

I remember reading about it in a series of excerpts from her book published in *Paris Match*. The publicity threw Picasso into such a fit of fury and despair it threatened to unhinge him, and his friends were hard pressed to calm him down. He tried to sue the publishers ... unless I am confusing this book with one written by Denyse Ouimet after her separation from Simenon, called *A Bird for the Cat*. The title refers to the way he hypnotized her, immobilized her with fear, paralyzed her with his predatorial regard as a cat mesmerizes its prey before pouncing.

Françoise Gilot was also a painter, but she gave it up to devote herself entirely to "the genius." When the urge to paint returned to her, she found herself confronted by the thunderings of that genius, who felt she had betrayed him. He told her she had to choose between him and her art. She took the next train, as well as Claude and Paloma.

There is a famous photograph of Paloma Picasso, taken by Helmut Newton, in which she appears bare-breasted, glass in hand, a very Spanish air about her. She was famous for being the daughter of a famous father. Françoise herself is still best known for having been Picasso's mistress. Her own paintings remain largely unviewed. Her fate resembles that of Camille Claudel, whose tragic life inspired a film Françoise may have seen. If so, she must have recognized it as a portrait of herself.

Was there a gun on the table? History is silent on the point.

Alex Colville, a Canadian painter who shares with Jean-Paul Riopelle a truly international reputation, produces a maximum of three paintings a year. His studio is impeccably tidy. No one is allowed into it to photograph him. Someone once told me he has a reproduction of Vermeer's *The Lacemaker* on one wall. Whenever he finishes a canvas, he has it photographed and shipped to his agent. His work owes its appeal to the canon of beauty established by classical painting, in particular the work of Piero della Francesca and his mathematical conception of painting based on the Golden Section. Colville's meticulous technique also recalls that of Georges Seurat. The colours of his palette are the same as those that were chosen by Renaissance painters for their watercolour frescoes. It has been said that

Colville's style places him squarely among the new figurative painters known as the Magic Realists. The major American practitioner of this is Andrew Wyeth, but in fact Colville's work is not much like Wyeth's at all; it is closer to that of Magritte, although in Colville it is reality itself that is ambiguous and not merely the relationship between the objects within the painting. The presence of animals and machines in some of his paintings, as well as his constant return to self-portaiture, could also place him in the realm of metaphysical realism whose atmosphere recalls that of certain compositions by Chirico.

One of Colville's best-known canvases shows him naked from the waist up, as Picasso is in many photographs. Colville is leaning in a door frame looking out over the ocean. In the foreground, a table with a revolver resting on it. The heavy contrast between the black metal revolver and the luminous warmth of the wooden table. It must be very hot; the scene reminds one of the Robert Capa photograph. When I imagine the photograph, I see the ocean again, this time without the parasol, only the summer wind on an afternoon in the 1950s. I still believe that people who leave revolvers lying about on tables are thinking about the ocean.

Postscriptum:

I have revised this text after seeing *Surviving Picasso*, the film inspired by Françoise Gilot's memoir. In it, Picasso is portrayed by Anthony Hopkins, and the film contains an unforgettable scene in which Dora Maar toys with a knife on a café table. Also after reading several recent biographies of Picasso, some of which relate the destructiveness that accompanied his genius, a destructiveness that survived even his death; after the publication by Taschen of a coffee-table book (sold everywhere at a ridiculous price) that perpetuates the myth; after a visit to the Picasso Museum to view an exhibit of works dedicated to him by David Hockney, who also idolized Picasso as a paternal figure; after a conversation between myself and someone who shared my indignation at the rift that exists between the art and the private life of this holy monster who dominated the world of twentieth-century art. I tell myself that, basically, Picasso has become yet another victim of the revisionism that has struck down all the great men of the century. As with Einstein, Freud, Marx, Joyce and Brecht, Picasso's relationship with women has been subjected to an exhaustive inquisition. The work that men leave behind them, work whose role is to embody them after

their inability to continue embodying themselves, is being scru-
tinized and weakened by a discourse that compromises any
chance of peace there might have been in this incessant war
that, as Marguerite Duras puts it, is inherent in the amorous and
problematic condition that exists between men and women.

Françoise Latour

THE RINGING of the telephone cuts through the heavy, thick air in the dog days of July. At the other end of the line, an English voice asks me in French if I know of an Acadian heroine who could lend her name to a perfume that her company is about to put on the market. Acadia has sold herself more than once, but her history is still sleeping peacefully in the deep woods and in the obedient clay, like a beautiful rug stored in the basement of our collective amnesia. I come up with the name Françoise Latour, and am suddenly overwhelmed by the memory of a whole slice of my life and the ten years that have passed since.

November was pounding the coast with powerful, rebellious waves. I was dying of love and boredom. Like the sea's liquid lace, my life was forming and dissolving and forming again more beautifully with each crashing wave. Packed in a nylon parka and waterproof boots, I strode along the beach, muttering to myself that there must be other locations, other beaches, other lives to stride through, other currents to swim against. We were making a film, *Madame Latour*, and I was well aware that it was a leaky ship on a troubled sea. I was trying to justify every decision, every shot, every subtlety, to a producer whose only goal was fame and fortune, who was obsessed with his own groundless conviction that emotions could spring from nothing and that everyone's life was exactly the same as everyone else's.

Françoise Latour was the wife of Charles de Saint-Étienne de Latour, governor of Acadia, a man who loved the land and did not believe in exploiting it by exterminating its animals for their fur, which would then be sacrificed to the greater glory of France. His insistence on befriending the New Englanders attracted the ire of the Court, which sent a new governor to replace him: Charles de Menou d'Aulnay, nephew of Cardinal Richelieu and a cruel and intransigent man with the soul of a technocrat. While Latour was away in Boston, d'Aulnay laid siege to the fort, which Françoise defended with her last ounce of strength. In the end, d'Aulnay hanged her supporters before her eyes, kept her away from her son and locked her in a cell where she soon died of rage and despair.

It's never a good idea to awaken the dead, but that's what we were trying to do that fall. It had already started to snow. We were at a standstill. We had lost our continuity. We had not been able to film the connecting scenes between the white sequences of winter and the browns of the dying autumn. Meanwhile, the actors played cards in their motel rooms, waiting for the temperature to drop and the leaden sky, which had brooded over us since the beginning of filming, to clear and show us its merciful stars. The ghost of Charles de Menou d'Aulnay stalked the land. His priestly, fanatical figure appeared at the most bizarre moments, his almost inaudible laughter came to us through the snow, through the cold, turned up in the camera, penetrated our deteriorating relationships and showed up in the skyrocketing costs of production.

The screening of the rushes convinced me that we were headed for disaster. I wanted a film that closed in on details; the producer wanted a movie shot from a distance, resulting in scenes in which the characters appeared completely unbelievable. I wanted to preserve the real voices of the real people by incorporating archival images, prints from the era, shots of the land that had borne witness to the real drama. The producer insisted we shoot every foot of the film. I wanted to quit, to flee, to escape from the whole unfortunate mess. Unlike me, he thought everything was going along magnificently; he was like one of those characters in a Werner Herzog film who leads an army down a hostile river so they can build an opera house in the jungle, dragging them all to their certain, absurd deaths by the obstinate force of his fanaticism.

I still can't watch that film without thinking that Françoise Latour deserved better than the Hollywooden treatment we gave her. We could have made her a true heroine, a charismatic leader, a lesson for those who look for reasons for our having lost so many wars, and accepted our historical disfiguration for the sake of the myth. Instead, all we made was a slapdash film whose only saving grace is the interpretation brought to the role by the principal actress, with whom I fell hopelessly in love; her limpid blue eyes as clear as the crashing waves are the only pleasant memory I have of that whole leaky enterprise.

When she cried, she was saying: "I am crying for her, I cry for everything she endured." In a way, she was also crying for us. We are the last act of that drawn-out drama, inheritors of that cold anger that must have spread through our soul like the incarnation of evil or grace that, combined with courage, can raise the ocean from its bed. If only we had retained a tiny fraction of their fervour, the knowledge that life can only be redeemed by the enormity of what it loses, by what it pays for whatever it believes in. Otherwise, what's the use of laying siege to anything, of stretching it out for as long as possible, as we do on those rare occasions when we carve our obsessions, like so many errors and regrets, into the false light of our age?

To this day I have never seen a perfume called Françoise Latour. Perhaps, after all this time, her tormentor is still denying her her place in history, a history he wants her to die in and us to forget.

Acadians in Montreal

THE PLANE from Moncton bellies up to Gate 5 at the
Dorval airport, which never fails to remind me of
just how far we've come. The last gate at the end of
a long corridor, Gate 5 is where domestic flights take off to the
country's most distant destinations. The only advantage to
landing here is the long walk we have to take through the terminal to the exit, which gives us time to wake up and settle into
our we're-not-from-Quebecitude. There was a time when this
realization caused me a great feeling of frustration, which
always brought on a deep sadness. We lend a sort of dignity to
our despair by adopting attitudes of irony and stoicism and,
sometimes, cynicism.

This particular morning I'm travelling with a colleague from work. Because we're early, we decide to make a small detour to visit a friend of hers who has recently moved to the big city.

She's a Buddhist. She has a small shrine set up in a corner of her bachelor apartment. She doesn't seem put out or even surprised by our unannounced visit, although it is barely eight o'clock in the morning. The conversation at the Formica table in her kitchen gravitates around meditation and a host of other Oriental subjects, and I do my best to stay awake.

The question comes up suddenly. Heavy, weighty, it arrives in a lead-lined box with carcinogenic sides, wafts in like a whiff of pollution, is dumped in our midst like a huge drop of acid rain. An off-hand question that appeals to our curiosity, but is driven in at a metaphysical, anguish-making slant, like cold autumn rain. A question marked Red Alert, a sort of Ground Zero of expectancy, a masterpiece of renunciation, a formal declaration of escape:

"So, what's happening in Moncton?"

Happening in Moncton. Happening. Moncton. Well, of course something must be happening in Moncton. One of the peculiarities of life is its tendency to renew itself by having something happen: a good day, a bad month, an indifferent year. But what is this thing that's happening? Life just going on? Jean-Guy Pilon once wrote, in an issue of *Liberté* devoted to Acadia, that "Moncton is so ugly its ugliness must be deliberate," meaning that it is inconceivable its citizens could have achieved such a horror by accident. The relationship between Acadia and Quebec has come to the point where either side can find whatever it needs to cobble together a hatred of or sympathy for the other's artistic or collective expression.

"So, what's happening in Moncton?"

Those who survived the plague lit candles every day in the shrine of the saint that delivered them from its scourge. Life replaces pride: they knew precisely how excellent their position would be when God drew up his final scoresheet. This woman is already part of the big city. At night, when she sees the revolving searchlight atop Place Ville-Marie she thinks of a lighthouse, and when she hears the roar of traffic she closes her eyes and remembers the ocean of her childhood summers. Life's everyday pleasures make her feel the images more intensely than the feelings that lie beneath them. She has given up speaking *chiac* and is giving herself over to *joual*. She no longer says "That's right nice" or "Don't worry your brain about it." She's part of French Canada now, having entered the linguistic limbo that precedes absorption into Quebecitude.

"So, what's happening in Moncton?"

Despite my incessant activity, my constant attempts to take stock of reality to the point where I risk alienating myself from it altogether, and, I suppose, my desire to maintain a certain poise, I suddenly become conscious of a profound and assumed otherness. I will always be a stranger in the eyes of those for whom the apotheosis of glory is to live anonymously in the heart of this city, this Montreal, this depository of all our resentment and all our unrealistic dreams.

Taxi Cormier makes a daily run between Caraquet and Montreal, and on it I once met a young man who had moved to the city to become a snowplow driver. For him, Montreal was always the biggest, its snow was always the deepest, its storms always dropped more megatons and its snow-removal equipment was always more than equal to the task. Back in Caraquet, his speech would become permanently self-referential, his sentences taking on the air of proverbs: "Do you even know who you're talking to?" Everyone knows that to drive a big snow-plow in the big city is to have found permanent favour in the eyes of the Eternal God.

"So, what's happening?"

So here she is, living day to day, getting by on EI, having her daily chats with Buddha, lost in her clouds of incense and invaded by the ceaseless white noise of a major North American city in which she tries to obliterate her ego, to lose her deeper self, all the time wondering if out there, out beyond the Jacques Cartier Bridge, there aren't other time zones, other worlds, other universes, if somewhere the intergalactic dust isn't sticking together in new ways to form new stars.

"So, what?"

So, not much. I moved a little farther from the university. My cat wandered off into the marsh and hasn't come back. The other day I went for a walk in Place Champlain, and you'll never guess whom I ran into. My mother's having her cataracts removed. Maurice sold his Tercel. Catherine quit her job. Marc bought a house. Jean-François is trying to get everyone to sign a petition to stop them from opening a massage parlour next to his house. Marcia planted a whole forest of rose bushes. Alain gave his best shoes away to some guy he met. Jean-Marie turned fifty. Gérald has gone to France. Josée's mother bought a restaurant. Roméo put an apartment in his basement for his daughter. Hermé sleeps all the time. In fact, he's sleeping now, snoring through this banal chronicle to which she listens with such an air of detachment, aware that nothing back home matches this urban feverishness in which it is such a good idea to believe.

I am asleep. I'm dreaming of a land where everyone is fulfilled by their differentness, where everyone has given up making comparisons and has banished all similes. A land where the only thing left to invent is rain.

Art and Life

THERE ARE only two survival strategies you need to remember: art and life. A simplistic notion that came to me from God knows where, which I trot out from time to time whenever it seems to fit the occasion. It's not a proposition that meets with a lot of approval in some circles, especially when coupled with the idea that women give life, whereas men appropriate language to themselves from some unresolvable anguish at the idea that they are going to die and that they, too, must leave some tangible proof behind of their passage on Earth. Women sometimes draw an unconscious security from their position of superiority, because life has designated them as essential carriers in a sort of nomadic paradigm that leaves no ruins and reinvents itself in the smoke of the next campfire. For men, the situation is less tenable because their works are subject to bad weather and the caprices of their fellow men. Very few works from the Greek texts have come down to us intact, and most of those that have are preserved like holy relics. We have to settle for clumsy reproductions if we want to feel even a shadow of the emotion that once caused people to break down and cry before the originals.

In the London Underground, a giraffe's head is the only indication that we are approaching the zoo. It's the first time I've let myself be dragged to it, because to me the saddest of all sights is that of caged animals, their captive state being an insult to the most elementary notion of liberty. We shuffle past cage after cage: a colony of monkeys, their backsides bleeding; a group of polar bears circling ponderously on their concrete ice pan, a flock of birds dazed by overpopulation in their native jungle. And suddenly, as we come to the orangutan cage, the verification of—or at least the formulating evidence for—my theory. It is still a vague idea, so diffuse that it is difficult to put my finger on it, but it has to do with this orangutan family, this couple, which is most likely two individuals thrown together to give visitors an impression of conjugal bliss. Whatever the case, it works. The female sits at the back of the cage, playing with her child, oblivious to the "Oohs" and "Ahhs" from the horde of visitors that file past, rapturizing on the universality of the maternal instinct. Near the front of the cage, the male sticks handfuls of straw on his head and makes faces, desperately trying to make the visitors look at him, too, or perhaps only at him. In the animal kingdom, life manages to go on without all the elegant theories we come up with to explain the mysteries of our origins or our perseverance, but I perceive in this naive and pitiable display the notions of art and life in their most elementary and moving dimensions.

Marion McCain once asked to meet me, but I had no intention of making the long drive to Florenceville, headquarters of the famous multinational food empire and home of one of the wealthiest families in the country, so she arranged for us to meet halfway, in Fredericton, on the day that I was to receive a prize for excellence in the cinematographic arts from the province's lieutenant-governor. In one of the rooms in the Beaverbrook Art Gallery, in the company of its director, me resplendent in my shiny new suit, she said she wanted me to curate an art exhibition that would bear her name. She was wearing a certain kind of metal bracelet. She emanated a natural elegance, the kind of effortless tact with which grown-ups listen indulgently to what is often being said offhandedly to them. I accepted the job. I had a year to put the show together. Despite the metal bracelet, it had not occurred to me that she wouldn't be around on the night of the opening. Her absence was written on the grave faces of many of the guests. I spoke briefly to a largely English audience, my words flopping between the two solitudes; I talked mostly about art and life, the fact that they are the only two strategies we need to survive. Marion McCain had lost life, but her work continued, and, thanks to her, these paintings, tangible as the walls that held them, would live in our minds until the end of time.

The infinite sweetness of an evening in July, the moon's halo mirrored in the still waters of a nearby bay. A light breeze stirs the scene, as do the cries of a child playing in the night with his birthday present, and the murmur of conversations punctuated by bursts of laughter and frequent pauses for more wine.

There is a charm about her that discourages any indiscretion arising from her beauty. She has the kind of strength that comes from the certain knowledge that she can restart her life whenever and wherever she wants, that she could live anywhere at all as long as she had her five children with her. It is a perspective that would send the most ardent suitor packing. I tell her that I have nothing to match it, my fragile world being made up only of incidents and having neither the mystery nor the range of a life that metamorphoses ceaselessly from one staggering enigma to another. A security against all threats.

The source of her serene assurance comes no doubt from her constant immersion in emotion and tenderness, this fountain of life that gurgles and regenerates itself ceaselessly. A woman beside her, who has no children of her own and wants none, tries to tell her that her theory makes no sense, that it is just the whim of an irremediably masculinized brain. But she hardly hears the woman's argument. She has turned towards the bay and is watching the implacable, eternal sea. The child in the distance stops playing, begs his mother to continue, insensitive to the signs of fatigue she is showing. Life, yes, but why this selfless art of women, springing from the deepest possible wells of generosity and discretion? Fragile, adaptable, effective and powerful, life thrusts aside everything that gets in its way.

The Road from Basel

P AUL OF TARSUS fell off his horse on the road to Damascus when he heard the voice of God saying to him: "Paul, Paul, why do you persecute me?"

We were passing through Basel, Switzerland, on our way to Budapest to see the National Museum of Fine Art, and decided to stop to visit a friend of a friend who was supposed to be an excellent cook. There were three of us in an ancient Peugeot 61, a bucket of bolts held together by rust. In the villages and especially on the interconnecting highways, it seemed to motor along with a will of its own, and when it accelerated to top speed it assumed the alarming aspect of a coffin on wheels.

But our love of travelling was stronger than our innate fear of death.

It was a Sunday afternoon. In the museum gift shop, I remember seeing a beautiful print of Jasper Johns's *Painting with Two Balls*, which I still kick myself for not buying; I told myself at the time that it would surely pop up again somewhere when I had more money, although I should have known that it was the kind of treasure that never surfaces twice. I was always being beset by beautiful and enticing objects I could never hope to afford.

Upon leaving the museum, we felt hungry, so we got back into the car to look for the road to the famous cook's house. With no directions, navigating in darkness and in a city with confusing street signs, the car, despite our vigorous protestations, turned the wrong way on a one-way street. The police, usually never very far away, stopped us immediately and took us to the station, where they made a thorough search of our possessions, including our passports, those incontrovertible and enigmatic elements of our identity.

With our very fragmentary knowledge of German, we were given to understand that the problem was that we needed to procure visas for Hungary and Czechoslovakia. At that time, the Iron Curtain was still drawn tightly and held fast. The discussion went on for an eternity, it seemed, until one of the police officers settled the matter by telling us that they would escort us to the border and that it would be in our best interest to not return through Switzerland. Their decision was based on an incontestable argument: our car was too dirty. Which, when we thought about it, made a certain amount of sense.

The car got us to Budapest before breaking down. I can still hear the insane laughter of the mechanic, standing under the hoist with his arms in the air, shaking with hilarity, obviously laughing at us, or at least at our vehicle, the word "Peugeot" frequently punctuating his Hungarian. At the same garage, a Canadian diplomat gave us some free advice about life in Hungary. Outside, the city smelled of coal smoke. It was winter, although there was no snow. The guards in the National Museum were all asleep. My hair was longer in those days.

On Reading Cendrars

I was already such a lousy poet

I didn't know how end it

A MAN is rocking his child to sleep in an apartment across from a cemetery. You need to know that the man is a walker. He walks all the time, and in the course of his peregrinations, all sorts of ideas come into his head: ideas about life, about art, about the paintings he could make, and, I would guess, about the illusions he nurses along the way. To get to the town he has to pass through the cemetery, then cross a large field, heavy with all the secrets of the world.

One night, in the cemetery among the crypts, an immense black dog crept up behind him, raised itself on its hind legs and pushed its front paws into his back. He still doesn't know if he dreamt it, but he felt his blood run cold as the dog's dark shadow ran off into the mysterious night, zigzagging in and out of the headstones and their own disquieting shadows.

A man rocks his daughter while reading aloud from a book she cannot possibly understand, asleep as she is in her father's steady voice. His voice becomes a probe in the apartment filled with all the sadness, the tears, the murmurs that come in through its too-thin walls. His voice follows his own ephemeral voyage as it meanders through time. The man reads. The poetry is new, still in the act of creating itself, the echo of an entire world that is awakening and discovering its own voice. It speaks of a river to cross, of a language to invent, of a dignity to reclaim. It speaks of love and endlessness.

When he tires of these complaints, the man puts down the book and opens another, older one, one that sustains his unfailing belief in the advisability of living in this century, a belief he needs in order to establish parameters and to consign within them his emotional fragility. "When I travel I want to close my eyes / To sleep / O how I would love to sleep." Cendrars or Apollinaire. *La Prose du Transsibérien* or *Alcools*. Who invented what before whom? "If you want prose, read a newspaper," a line written long before Duchamp scrawled his signature on a urinal and changed forever the art of a century that was born to make its statement in favour of life. Poetry as genial intuition, as first awakening.

Later, the father will learn that it was Cendrars who invented the kind of spontaneous prose seen later in the work of Louis-Ferdinand Céline, and, in the U.S., of Jack Kerouac, who said that all he wanted his books to do was "shore up Céline and Joyce."

The father's voice becomes music. He reads *The Drunken Boat* and wonders how to reconcile Rimbaud's music with the intonations of those poets whose journeys took them against the current of their century. How to flee, to endure, to shore up this music, to make words become real, like flesh, like the flash of distress signals. How to make our own contributions notable rather than negligible, or, as so often happens, negligent.

Crayons

THERE IS a stack of planks in front of our house, piled to form a kind of triangular cabin so that they will dry for some future construction project. The logs had been bought and taken to the sawmill to be sawn, and now they wait in our yard, transformed into planks upon which the summer heat will do its work. My mother has gone to Caraquet. She went to buy me some crayons. I know she also has other reasons, but in my mind she's making the trip just for me, to bring me some crayons. I can smell them already. It is another interminable and significant childhood summer in the 1950s.

I would go into raptures over the colouring books in Robichaud's five-and-dime. Could I ever hope to achieve such mastery? To have that sureness, that precision, that elegance of treatment and liveliness of line? I was so paralyzed by their perfection that I couldn't bring myself to mar the cheap paper on which these masterworks had been printed by actually trying to colour them.

One of my childhood friends had learned to put a thin coat of very fine wax in the space to be coloured and then to outline it more intensely with the same crayon. I was bowled over by his expertise, his delicacy. He had discovered a style and an innovation, the subtlety of which rivalled that of Fra Angelico. He aimed no higher; he had found his métier and was happy to go on with his self-satisfying demonstrations, content to do it with different colours and wait for the miracle to unfold. I envied his ability, his style.

I, too, had mastered the art of colouring inside the lines of the drawing. But unlike my friend, having once demonstrated my prowess, I wanted to push it further. That summer I intended to work on the notion of perspective, to try to make the third dimension leap out of the second by the use of shad-

owing. I hammered away at this profound research and succeeded in discovering a much deeper motherlode, a level that
encompasses the very notion of painting itself and, along with
the use of light, gives the work the intangible and impregnable
quality, if not of real life, then certainly of the specific space
contained within the work itself. Colour would be the focus of
my preoccupations.

I noticed that pigment had density and that each colour
obeyed a strict code of fragility and resistance that determined
its order of precedence in application. Red over yellow, blue
over red. You could mix all the colours until you got black,
which nullified all hope of further layerings. I shared the results
of my experiments with the children I knew and succeeded in
holding their attention, at least for as long as the demonstrations took place, but there were few comments following my
scholarly presentations.

In a space lit by two luminous trees of quartz lamps, an artist
still works at remaking colour the way ice is remade between
glacial periods. He's come a long way since that summer in the
1950s when he knew nothing of Pollock's drippings, the torn
canvases of Fontana or the black-and-white abstractions of

Borduas, when he amused himself with wax crayons in a triangular cabin of planks drying in the sun. Of course, he is still fascinated by those tiered boxes, each tier a range of pointed coloured missiles, but it has never occurred to him to try to make serious art with them. He has been told that their pigment is unstable and that he must work for posterity. They are objects whose beauty is sufficient unto themselves, and fascination with them is a form of remembrance of things past.

This fascination and transformation. Colour comes into its own again with Renoir, Matisse or Warhol; the drawings of Dine, Hockney or Beuys; the paintings of Johns, Tàpies or Twombly. Yet they all see things with the same eyes. What, then, is happening? If only we could see as we saw for the first time, understand words the way we did when they first came to us, vibrant with mystery and glistening with newness, the intensity of those first sensations serving as a refuge, then no doubt we could forget meaning and concentrate on the brilliance of living in total intensity.

This disturbance and this reinvention. We who come from the colonies wait for news from the capital, living fitful and ill-tempered lives in the grip of forces that disarm and limit us. We should wield our crayons in protest against the tyranny of the masterpiece. The transient should be our code. But sooner or later we must negotiate the troubled waters in which the serene intimacy of childhood encounters the terrorism of ideologies.

One day I met a woman whose perfume reminded me of those crayons. I told her about it, without elaborating, thinking I was paying her the greatest compliment I had ever given anyone. Being near her was a sort of return to fresh, new sensations, to those summers when the grass was high and a peculiar shade of blue-green. When nature was an earthly paradise where one could, when all else failed, go and hide. Later, she bought three crayons and gave them to me in a clear plastic box, which was nothing like those orange-yellow boxes the Crayola company still makes. Each stick was made of three harmonized colours whose proportions I could never quite get right. Their smell alone fascinates me; I still can't escape from the spell that makes these simple objects the fetishes of an obsession and a longing whose mystery dissolves in the telling.

The Crayola company has recently put on the market a new kind of crayon whose pigment is more concentrated and the matrix softer. These have the potential to produce superb and lasting drawings. After all these years, perhaps it is time to resume my research into colour, interrupted not so long ago by a course of study a little too monopolized by art history. I was taken over by the myth of those who expect consequence and gain, and who insist on being told what to buy and what profits to hope for.

L'Air du Temps

IN THOSE days, I could score a metro ticket with my thumbnail, make little flanges along the edges and fold it into a small box. I'd also taught myself to cut down Styrofoam cups with my teeth, making a series of rings I took particular care not to break. I took photographs towards an anthropology of contemporary life: for example, of the way you hold yourself when you crave a cigarette. I spray-painted orange-coloured canvases with essence of orange in order to prove that snow is white and the sky is blue. With my right hand, I tied a shoelace around my left and pulled until the left hand went into spasms, thus proving its inferiority. I took photographs of every photographable part of my body to create a sort of geography of my own landscape. I wanted to sell line drawings by the linear foot, paintings by the square foot, sculptures by the pound, gestures by the second and imprints of my hand. I believed that to be an artist meant cranking out imitations of immortality. I would photograph the sky above the city on the theory that the images provided proof that twenty minutes of my life had been irrevocably lost. I wanted to sign blow-ups of my signature. I traced details from photographs and exhibited them next to the originals under tracing paper. I superimposed the image of my face on the words of a popular song. I made stamps commemorating my own work, postcards commemorating my paintings and memento mori commemorating my death. I picked junk off the streets, took photographs of the sidewalks, and then put the junk back and took more photographs, for a sequence of before-and-after shots. I separated the plies in sheets of Kleenex and catalogued them in archival detail. I wrote scholarly texts on the stated versus the intended aims of people who masturbated under platforms. I attended conferences at which the speakers climbed up on tables, thrust their hands into their underwear and ejaculated handfuls of confetti through their flies, shouting, "Sperm! Sperm!" I organized

contests featuring fake prizes and meals of all-you-can-eat tour-
tière. I published collections of insults, of exercises to do in the
nude. I became haunted by the image of a tiger leaping upon a
woman, always the same woman, eating, running and dreaming
with her. Her perfume was L'Air du Temps by Nina Ricci, her
eyes were like foliage, her laughter explosive and dangerous. It
was when Riopelle came to visit us, when I ran into Barthes at
the Hautes Études, when I saw Deleuze in Vincennes, Lévi-
Strauss at the Collège de France. It was the smell of Gitanes in
the air port lounge and later in Paris, where we were all geniuses
together (yes, yes, Aznavour), with fire in our bellies and a life-
time to kill.

Lyrical Abstraction

rt in Europe Since 1945 is a small, inoffensive book I picked up at a rummage sale, with reproductions illustrating a modernity that was called "Abstract Expressionism in the United States" and "Abstract Lyricism in Europe."

I loved Hans Hartung's black clouds, Jean-Paul Riopelle's multicoloured forests, Lucio Fontana's black holes, Antoni Tàpies's graffiti, Nicolas de Staël's extreme landscapes. Their names have practically disappeared from the history of art. For a while now.

Beyond the ocean, it seemed, was a country in the process of defying a continent, a universe. It was the post-war period.

Paranoiacs had the CIA plotting the destabilization and control of Europe by bombarding it, through its artists and intellectuals, with ideologies that sooner or later would topple governments. Culture as a weapon, seduction as a form of combat.

I also liked the energized lines of Jackson Pollock, the taut lines of Franz Kline, the minimal lines of Robert Motherwell, the coloured lines of Clyfford Still, the tangled lines of Arshile Gorky. Lines: the supremacy of the drawing over the mass, over the full brush. The blueprint was more important than the completed building. Primitive art, an extension of colouring. What makes a great painting great is always light. Jasper Johns's electric light bulb.

I did not like Mark Rothko's melting forms or Barnett Newman's coloured fields or Helen Frankenthaler's iris-like veils. I painted in basement stones to look like cakes, not unlike Claes Oldenburg. I attended an English university. The professor whose influence on me was decisive was a transplanted American from UCLA who liked Rothko's sobriety, Newman's cold analyticism, Frankenthaler's enthusiasm. All the rest were losers, he said, don't even look at them. In the war of "isms," their case was being re-evaluated. You had to be patient.

———

History could not be hurried. It had its own pace, its own rhythm.

It was the '60s, post-war itself was an unfortunate abstraction, a *refus global* of which we were the rebellious products. You had to live in the here and now in order to survive into the future, you had to live in your own time if you wanted to live for a long time.

Art isn't about fashion, it's about emotion. There's a twenty-year gap between 1950 and 1970. The old cliché: What's twenty years in the history of humanity? A single generation. There'll be others. Put the world back in perspective and try to see the future as the improbable prolongation of the past. Those are the kinds of conclusions you come to when you say that time is not an arrow but a pulse.

A Duchamp Retrospective

THE ROADS frozen all the way to the Tennessee border, in a van bought from a guy in Memramcook,
with a complicated arrangement of beds in the back
so that two of us could sleep while the other two drove, like a
long relay race, Louisiana, the St. Martinville museum, the
magical Marie Laveau, the guide who extolled the benefits of
the Deportation, the oak under which Évangéline bestowed her
final kiss, the air heavy and as translucent as the glassine green-
ery on the postcards, the rubby who recommended we drink a
bottle of Mad Dog for the experience, which we did, then New
Orleans, its tourist traps, the ancient black jazz musicians at
Preservation Hall, the oyster bars, the red lights spilling blood

over the city, the Hurricanes at Pat O'Brien's bar, the $65-a-glass drinks that a group of students on vacation, sitting at a round table, sipped through straws, a ritual involving a lot of slurping and bubbling through the pink, syrupy concoction, the heaters heating the sidewalk cafés, Christmas night with the single last-minute decoration, the crayfish scuttling in circles in the boiling water, Cajuns dancing, the music evincing a sombre, silvery sexuality, the hotels on Miami Beach like decadent music, her mauve swimsuit and, when she stood up, every eye on the beach rising with her, her body a mantra, a gateway into dreams, the intoxicating smell of her suntan lotion mixed with perfume mixed with sweat, the Iroquois Hotel in New York, the black-and-white TV, the horizontal line that kept jumping across the screen, the cold air that rippled the polyester lace curtains, the dirty windows, the blurry city, the slovenliness of the boy in the elevator, his ghetto blaster, his arrogance, that night seven people murdered in the city, a quiet New Year's Eve according to the newscasts. Then at last the Museum of Modern Art, Dali's *Persistence of Time*, Mondrian's *Broadway Boogie-Woogie*, Monet's *Water Lilies*, all leading up to the Marcel Duchamp Retrospective, Duchamp being one of the three most important artists of the century, the others Picasso and Matisse, all French, well, nearly, decline as a source of inspiration. For dust on a sheet of glass, for uniforms drawn with lead thread, for Parisian air in a bottle, drawings turning on a turntable, a star-shaped tonsure, commonplace objects elevated to the level of art by having been signed, stalemated chess games, people exploding in stairways. Seminal works, works that make other works possible, striking and provocative and fascinating enigmas. A mouse cage filled with marble cubes made to look like cubes of sugar. "Why Not Sneeze Rose Sélavy?" A curious title from one who, smiling behind his cigar, speaks almost no English and cuts us loose in a meaningless world.

Malraux

oncton. *The Palace Grill.*

As you went in you saw a series of photographs on the wall behind the counter, the owner with various celebrities of the day. Miss Canada, Stan Mikita, *you name it.*

On the other walls were the landscapes that were de rigueur in every Chinese restaurant, embroidered in rich, glitzy-coloured thread, *sweet and sour.*

The tables were cunningly arranged to create little cozies or alcoves. They were made of imitation-wood melamine.

You could go up a step and enter a completely dark room, the sun no more than a distant rumour. After a few minutes,

when your eyes adjusted to the gloom, you could order a drink
and while away the time it took for the beer to make its slow
descent from glass to porcelain.

I was in there one day with a friend who had just come back
from Europe. I hadn't done much travelling and I listened to
him as though he were a modern-day Marco Polo. The women,
the bizarre habits and customs of the people he'd met, people
who spoke our language and whose existence was known to us
from the grey, tortured films we watched when we got home
at night, drunk, from our eternal, nocturnal wanderings. He
hadn't picked up an accent. He was the only person I knew
who'd gone away and come back without denigrating himself
for having become such a vulgar American.

At Christmas he'd gone to Mexico to see Ivan Illich and
came back convinced that he would never make a revolution-
ary, not him, and that the only hope of salvation was in perpetual departure, all revolutions having failed, leaving nothing to
do but wander about continually, trying to close the circle of
the countryless existence he had sworn to adopt.

Nothing would get between him and life except the world
and its miracles.

I had been sick. Three weeks in a hospital, alone, reading Malraux's *La Condition humaine*. My room looked out over a four-lane highway, and at night the cars' headlights, like Chinese lanterns, traced shadows across my walls. I had been separated from a lover for the whole time of my illness. The unforgettable memory of her return, grief like an obsession with pain. The scene in which they divide up the cyanide. There is no love in that novel. A story of men who die for their principles, political or otherwise. What makes a great book? Its slender outline in the room, her words distorted in the funhouse mirror of her tears, and my life coming apart throughout the long nights among those strange silhouettes projected by car headlights on the walls of my room. Rewinding the film of my life, fast-forwarding the film of my life.

And I wanted to write books.

Nixon's first trip to establish diplomatic relations with the People's Republic of China.

Suddenly, China was everywhere, in all the magazines, the glossy paper tigers of the West.

Somewhere in my memory there's that painting by Les Levine based on a photograph showing Nixon eating with a group of Chinese dignitaries, making much of his unfamiliarity with their food, his evident discomfort at the idea of eating with chopsticks, his body language shouting what he would never allow himself to articulate otherwise.

In another magnificent photograph, we see him sitting on the deck of a boat—the majestic Yangze River in the background in all its eternal serenity, grey as a wash in Chinese ink—surrounded by all those beatific Chinese faces, the Americans looking like beings from another planet. Nixon's pinched face. An alert to the underground shelters. Could we even imagine him swimming with his closest henchmen in the waters of the Mississippi?

Who knew that one day he would be dethroned over a boring affair of electronic eavesdropping concocted by a band of incompetent plumbers?

The weather was good that afternoon, the inner calm of an old photograph floating tranquilly and silently down the river . . .

In the silence that descends between courses.

Paris. Cité universitaire. Germany House.

On her wall was a photograph, taken around the turn of the century, of a young prostitute in a Chinese brothel. She said it reminded her somehow of Germany, with its graffiti aimed at anyone who opposed the Baader-Meinhoff group.

Kristeva. She learned Chinese in order to go there.

Barthes came back disappointed.

We bought posters of the Chinese Revolution. For a long time I had one pinned on the wall of my room, something to look at when I had nothing better to do and needed to convince myself that I was doing something essential and important. The image, printed on cheap paper, was of a group of smiling peasants crossing a bridge. It made me think of the lurid illustrations in my old school textbooks. I would gaze at them for hours, drift off into whole adventures, pour myself into their endless daydreams.

What does it really mean to want, to have, to keep or to defend one's faith?

China, ever and always an inexhaustible book of wonders, the kind of book you would gladly go to prison for, just for succumbing too deeply to its dreams.

In China at that time there were no art galleries, nothing like a cultural industry. Nothing but the artless production of icons, votive offerings. Graven images.

Later, Kristeva, back in the United States at Columbia University, deplored the artlessness of Americans, which she ought to have found a lot more tolerable than that of the Chinese.

Why is Europe always looking for new lands to conquer, new naïvetés to analyze?

What does it really mean to have faith?

Paris. Not far from the Luxembourg metro.

In a restaurant called L'Empire Céleste, telling ourselves that Françoise Mallet-Joris lived right there, right across the street. The name of the restaurant was the title of one of her books.

The menu was a mimeographed sheet, and the Chinese waiters wrote our orders on the paper tablecloths. Customers had to make up their own bills, and the Muscadet was goodish and cheap. One Chinese New Year's Eve we went there because we wanted to do something special to celebrate the occasion. It was open as usual. Nothing changed. After the meal we wished the staff a happy new year, but they barely acknowledged even hearing us. No mixing of cultures here, was the message. Even in the West, the Silk Road keeps its secrets.

Those who have read Françoise Mallet-Joris's work will no doubt know if it's true about the mixing of cultures, but since none of us had read a single one of her books, I couldn't say one way or the other. All I knew were the songs she had written for Marie-Paule Belle, but I doubt that what Malraux wrote about China after spending so much time there had much in common with this China she could see from her apartment window across the street, or with what we saw in the restaurant's dining room. Whatever it was, it remained a mystery.

"When one sets out, the other comes back."

I returned to the L'Empire Céleste one cold, rainy January night in 1980. I was alone. At the table next to mine, a group of people were talking about computers, arguing about the age at which children become better at using them than we ever could. They were in awe of the kind of genius that could extrapolate secrets from gross matter.

The waiter still took down my order on the tablecloth, and the room, though drained of its sense of mystery, still resounded with the noise of conversations whose echoes were distorted in the faint reflection of the mother-of-pearl mosaics that decorated the restaurant walls.

But who really cares about all that?

Paris. Cité universitaire. Canada House.

One morning I heard on the radio that Chairman Mao had celebrated the Chinese New Year by writing down the names of his closest collaborators in Chinese ideograms.

I was seized by the idea of writing the names of my closest friends in a way that would reflect the essence of each of them, capture their resonance, inject a portrait of them into the writing. I wrote her name in watercolour, since she was my closest friend, my most amazing and precious collaborator. I wanted to write the names of all my friends, everyone I loved, to see if, in the tracing of the letters that comprised their names, I would discover the essence of their places in my heart.

In the end I wrote only that one name, yours, in pink,

yellow and blue, as beautiful as those hearts by Jim Dine that, all during that time, remained imprinted on my eyes, in my mind and in my memory after I had seen them on the walls of the Sonnabend Gallery.

I sold it. I sold your name. The person who took it never paid me. I think now that that is the only appropriate way to part with the things we love and to which we are still too attached, believing that by having the thing we have some part of the person who inspired it.

We should only give away the things we love. The man who took it brought it back because he couldn't pay for it. Maybe he stopped loving it.

Money sometimes comes in handy as an excuse.

Montreal. Somewhere on rue Saint-Denis.

In one of the shops. This was some time after I had abandoned reality and was busy losing myself in images.

We were emerging from a long period of sadness. I had given up so many words, having first emptied them of their subtle meanings, drained them of their colours.

And the world hadn't stopped coming unglued either, or also, take your pick.

In this boutique I was taking photographs of embroidered silk kimonos.

Five years later I developed the film and enlarged the prints. I was surprised at how ordinary the images were. They were like the illuminated plastic statue of the Sacred Heart of Jesus that I had once found so beautiful but now thought of as trite, banal. In the interim I had realized that the memory of things is nothing more than a line crossed between faith and complexity. The charm is in its explication.

Five years later. I can't help thinking of the story of a group of mountain climbers killed in an avalanche, whose bodies were not found for fifty years. Their cameras were still intact. When the film was developed, it contained images of the climbers' dying agonies. Their suffering made immediate.

Time changes the way we see.

Moncton. The Rice Bowl Restaurant.

On Mountain Road, across from the liquor store, which is

its chief recommendation, according to one of my friends who lived in the area.

There are families with children of flawless candour who carry within their hearts a genetic and imperishable China.

An overwhelming vision when you are dying of hunger, and they are dying of alienation, boredom and exploitation.

It can't be as bad as we think it is. It can always get worse.

You have to die of something.

It's still the best food in town . . .

The cheapest . . .

The fastest.

In this takeout restaurant, as in the laundry formerly at the corner of Cameron and Saint-George, also run by a Chinese family, I have seen apparitions and illuminations, as in books of images of saints. I believe in the Rice Bowl as a sanctuary, a planned space at the heart of the city, an unfillable reservoir of sadness.

Outside, the rusted sign swings in the wind, its dragon coughing and spitting fire into the cold air of a North American winter. A numbness cramps my fingers when I take off my gloves to make these notes on the essential and the unchangeable.

Every word is worth its weight in gold.

Then they all go back to work, to their real work, leaving us here, alone in the palace of memories.

Without having seen a single wonder.

Bloodwork

PHOTOGRAPHS OF naked human bodies smeared with offal, penises wrapped in bandages, animals with their skin peeled back and their intestines being ripped out, sausages held genital high and sliced off in a bloody castration ritual, and blood, blood everywhere. Such were the activities of the Herman Nitsch group. The photographs were badly taken but nonetheless unforgettable and highly provocative.

Carole Laure, in the making of Dusan Makavejev's film *Sweet Movie*, presses a penis to her cheek. When the film came out, she threatened to sue the producers, saying the scene had not been in the original script. The film contained a number of other sequences shot in collaboration with the Nitsch group.

It was cold in Vienna that winter. An image stays with me, a prostitute suddenly caught in the headlights of the car, somewhere just off the Mariahilferstrasse. She was dressed in a red miniskirt and looked like a crucifixion against a building that divided the street. I couldn't meet Nitsch because the performances had so shocked the Viennese public that he had had to flee to Berlin.

In a gallery that sold his work, a blonde woman in a very elegant designer outfit gave me his address after showing me his work, which she handled with the greatest respect, holding each object as though it were a precious religious icon.

Les Levine has said that art galleries have become dumping grounds for outmoded communications systems. Is the body also now in the process of proclaiming its uselessness, given all the technological bits that are replacing it, part by part? The body, after all, produces nothing but sensations, which come to us through breaches in the wall of folly, error and decongestion. Is art still a useful barometer of future change, or is it being deregulated, perverted by its own system? Is art still the best way we have of expressing our emotions?

I was working on an article on the concept of merchandise

in the art marketplace. Herman Nitsch challenged the system by selling photographs whose quality was obviously second-rate, as though to show that photography as an artistic medium was already a hold-over from a bygone era. He thought of himself as an actor whose performances were recorded on film, and he thus represented an enigma to me, a living example of a market that, while purporting to reinvent itself, still had room for whatever anyone put into it. If art was dead, and he had no doubt it was, why hang its corpse on the walls of the middle class? All that mattered was to respect the first rule of the game: limit production to increase demand.

I recently came across Herman Nitsch on the walls of a museum, framed with all the trappings of mummification of which museums are capable. One of the works was a huge bloodstain. There was something written on it, I think; I no longer remember what it was. What I do remember is the blood, a burgundy splotch turning brown at the edges. Organic (I almost wrote orgasmic) pigments are difficult to stabilize, but the curators had done their best. All revolutions end up finding their true measures and their definitive resting places.

This morning I cut my little finger. I put a Band-Aid on it, but the perforated polyethylene strip with its small pad of cotton covered with thin Cellophane was not enough to staunch the blood that still oozes through the holes and stains the paper I'm writing on. It's not art. It's just blood. But if I sign it, cover it in Plexiglas, put it on an acid-free board and hang it on a museum wall . . . who's to say?

I remember Gina Pane's blood. During one performance, she cut her palm with a razor blade, and afterwards handkerchiefs stained with her blood were sold in packets, along with colour photographs of the performance. (David Douglas Duncan, one of the most celebrated of American war photographers, refused to shoot in colour because of the blood; its redness, he said, violated the decency of the battlefield.) During one of her performances, entitled "Van Gogh's Ear," Gina Pane repeatedly slashed her own ear. She also sold her used tampons. Blood as art material. She agreed to meet me in the well-appointed and elegant confines of the Stadler Gallery, which specialized in the sale of her work. Her speech was contrived. It annoyed her that her work was associated with the idea that, in our era, blood was tied in with the notion of ransom, that she was some kind of Christ shedding her blood to redeem our sins.

She mentioned that in the Middle Ages people thought blood was the vessel of life and its loss or contamination brought on all the diseases that flesh is heir to. An idea, she said, that would apply to our era as well.

I continued my research. Sometime later I met Michel Journiac, who celebrated a mass in which the faithful took communion by eating a slice of black pudding made from his own blood. Again, in the Middle Ages, sacrilegious masses were held in which newborn babies were sacrificed when the Devil was loose, and witches daubed themselves with their own excrement after having intercourse with him on a sabbath when he appeared in the form of a stinking goat.

Some time ago I thought of making a print from a series of photographs of myself extracting a syringeful of blood from my arm; I would use the blood to make stains on a number of small white cotton squares, and the photos would be reproduced leaving one empty space, where I would glue on one of the blood-stained squares. I got the idea after seeing, on the back of a religious picture, a small red dot on a tiny piece of tissue indicating that the picture had been touched to the heart of Brother André. In the same way, but different, my print would also have touched my heart. It would be a unique testament; it would also contain my DNA, with which someone someday could clone me as they are now learning to do with dinosaurs. We know there is still a strong connection between art and magic; the signature has taken the place of the fetish, especially if it is written in blood, the only ink that matters in contracts with the Devil. Faust's, for example. Faust should have been smart enough to save some of his blood and will his DNA to future scientists, requiring them to loop-clone him over and over again until the end of time.

In his performances, Nitsch used blood as a prop, pouring it in buckets over the celebrants of his Dionysian masses. I wonder how he kept it from coagulating? I remember my mother had to cook blood when it was still fresh, as soon as the pig was slaughtered and bled at the end of autumn, its raucous cries ringing through the village, the red changing to pink when it hit the snow, the smell of blood pudding filling the house when I came home from school, and sharing what we had with our neighbours, all of us renewed by the animal's blood. Perhaps it was because of this that I was fascinated by Nitsch's work, even though he used blood much more dramatically than we ever did in our village. Perhaps he made do with coloured water or red wine, as Christians do.

His was no anguished, overly dramatized solitude, as was the case with Gina Pane. No mutilation. For her, the re-enactment of ritual sacrifices, tracing the parabola of pain, was the ultimate verification of her existence. Her blood reclaimed its expiatory virtues from the great Christian tradition.

In zoos, animals mutilate themselves in their inconsolable despair at being kept in cages. The salt lick of blood. Blood is the only liquid that runs down the body without your really being aware of it, if it is your own. You have to see its crimson colour before you realize what it is. But the red eventually fades to brown, which, unless treated with a fixative, is an earth tone that disappears when washed.

I imagine one of Herman Nitsch's performers, after taking a shower, saying how happy he is to be rid of the smell and colour of blood, and the roughness of his clothes when it begins to dry. Smoking a cigarette in his white terry cloth bathrobe, saying there must be a better way to make a living than by celebrating this outmoded mass for the benefit of unbelievers in need of something resembling passion or snobs looking for something interesting to talk about.

In the meantime, there is no shortage of art historians, art critics, art collectors, art gallery owners, art conservators, art curators and art journalists who are happy to extract some meaning from all this bloodwork. Perhaps, in the end, they'll find it in the deep, inexhaustible strata where the subconscious crouches, waiting to crawl towards its ultimate and often troubling insertion into our daily lives.

Richard Lacroix

T HAT WINTER, bombs were going off in Montreal.
"The winter of our discontent," to borrow an out-
of-context line from Shakespeare. The School of
Fine Arts was closed, its mouldings mouldering in the sun
on Sherbrooke Street. The Graphic Guild, a print workshop
founded by Richard Lacroix, had become a refuge for all the
young dissidents imbued with their own modernity, having
found in Lacroix a convivial father figure who encouraged them
in their rebelliousness and consoled them in their confusion.

Shortly after they closed the school, I stopped in on my way
to Paris. I had a place on Aylmer, just above Sherbrooke, where
all the expensive stores belonged to rich Anglophones and

were, therefore, the frequent and appealing targets of the bombers.

Richard Lacroix was just back from Paris, where he had met with the historian Yves Robillard. Together, they had founded the Fusion des arts movement, the aim of which was to produce events that mostly had to do with kinetic art. I had read about the Graphic Guild in a small catalogue of reproductions put out for prospective customers. I went in, haggard and ill at ease, and found a place that would allow me to learn and explore a highly subversive technique. There were times when anyone who owned a printing press was subjected to certain controls by the police. When I showed Lacroix a bundle of drawings I'd made on a typewriter, he told me I had talent and went on to talk about life in general. The only thing I remember about our discussion is that, according to him, certain people consider themselves rich when they have little, while others think they are poor when they have a lot.

Over time, I noticed he was not all that interested in printmaking. His work focussed on art as a form of activism, as a political statement. He pushed a new kind of artist to the forefront: very urban, very New York, but originating in or harkening back to Europe. His printmaking, silk screens for the most part, had become a canned, pre-packaged tool of his enterprise, much as it was for Warhol in New York.

Although their paths seemed parallel at first, Lacroix and Warhol ended up going in totally different directions. Warhol became Warhol, and Lacroix became a print-seller. The last time I saw him, he was running across a street, his hair cut short, a fringe of beard on his chin, a leather vest, the very opposite of the dishevelled-rebel look he had affected when I knew him, when he had sat in his studio like *Aristide Bruant in His Cabaret*, to quote the title of the famous lithograph by Toulouse-Lautrec.

France and the States. Why is it always them? What happens when we paddle across the ocean of amnesia that divides and obsesses us?

La Patrie

AURÈLE ALBERT, postmaster, manager of the local bowling alley and Liberal organizer for the village of Saint-Simon, is sitting beside his wood stove. In his hand he holds a small black notebook that he carries with him at all times; in it, he has written the exact date upon which each of us is going to die. He has just made this public announcement, and we are all stunned by this revelation of his new shamanic powers.

Another childhood winter. It's after six o'clock and long dark, but we are still in the post office waiting for the mail, which has to come all the way from Caraquet. I'm not expecting a letter or a package, I'm waiting for a newspaper from Quebec: *La Patrie*.

The weekly comes in four sections, but the only one that interests me is the one that contains a reproduction of a colour photograph of a hockey player, almost always a Montreal Canadien, taken in a studio in front of a backdrop that is usually pale blue to make a nice contrast with the player's vermilion uniform. I don't always recognize the player's name, I'm not such a great Habs fan, but I am interested in colour. When I get home, I'll cut out the photo and paste it into a scrapbook I keep, along with photos of other athletes of the day, including boxers.

It's the heyday of Yvon Durelle, the fisherman from Baie Sainte-Anne who has become a symbol of the combative spirit of resistance for an entire people. Durelle—his very name suggests hardness and endurance—can stand up while taking punches, like Rocky Marciano, until his opponents are so exhausted that, with a good, solid right, he sends them crashing to the mat. He has done this often enough to earn a shot at the middleweight title against the foxy veteran Archie Moore. Durelle failed to defeat his adversary twice, but at least he managed to knock Moore down. *L'Évangéline*, the Acadian daily that went out of business in 1986, six months before its hundredth year of publication, followed the saga day by day until the photographs became too big to fit into my scrapbook.

La Patrie, however, wasn't that interested in Durelle. Each to his own hero. In Quebec, stardom is a societal phenomenon, a team thing. Here in Acadia, it's more individualistic, an intense and simple expression of the lone warrior struggling against unforeseeable odds. How long can he take the beating before he either delivers or receives the final blow?

We walk home in the dark with our precious booty, one of the thirty copies of *La Patrie* that arrive most Mondays and never on time. We are on a road that will not be cleared of snow until spring. Sometimes we climb up on the banks illuminated by the icy moon, so we can see the twinkling lights from distant houses hanging from the sky by threads of white smoke from wood stoves that never go out.

The hollow sound of our boots on the hard snow. It's the 1950s. We haven't done our homework. We eat our suppers listening to the radio, which comes from the Gaspé. A hockey game, maybe, or Marcel Martel singing *Un coin du ciel on vivra tous deux ma chérie*, over and over again. My brother paints on bits of old bedsheets with brushes he made himself from dog hair. I hang around watching the images emerge, aware that he has forbidden me to touch his paints, twelve pots of them with the image of a dog on each lid. Later, I learn that it is a greyhound, the logo of the Reeves company, named for the man who first put paint in tubes, enabling the Impressionists to get out of their studios and paint from nature.

The ritual of reading. First, look at the pictures, then read the captions under them, then the comics. That's enough for tonight, time to sleep. I still haven't done my homework. I'll think of an excuse tomorrow on the way to school. Since there is one teacher for all subjects from grades four to eight, there's a good chance she won't ask me for my homework or show the slightest interest in my intellectual development. Although I know that Konrad Adenauer is the Chancellor of West Germany, that Montcalm was defeated by Wolfe on the Plains of Abraham and that Dickey Moore is this week's featured player in *La Patrie*, I am more or less an autodidact, living in total ignorance of my own history, unable to see the deeper meaning behind the photo of Yvon Durelle lying stretched out on the mat. An image of defeat and the inevitable conclusion that exile is the only solution. Say goodbye to these long, interminable summers, all our people leaving and returning, they, too, with the image of Durelle lying on the mat, vaguely aware that their endless flight and irrevocable sadness may have something to do with this photograph in *La Patrie*.

Under the able coaching of Toe Blake, the Habs once again win the Stanley Cup. They are a well-oiled machine, fuelled as they are by a steady supply of players from Acadia, including Maurice and Henri Richard, and Jean Beliveau. Especially Maurice Richard, whose touch can heal the blind and cause the lame to walk. In the crackly voice of CHNC New Carlisle, we hear news of the riots following his suspension by league president Clarence Campbell. Quebec rising from its long winter, awakening from its long hibernation.

It's Easter week, school is a distant memory and winter lasts forever. We are too young to draw the lines and make the choices that come between the world and our images of it. We kneel in the mud and pray that our souls will be saved from the many sins that tempt us. Is our submissiveness not proof of our guilt? We take all of our direction from the Mass; we know that

God loves us because he never stops testing us. While we wait, we hide behind our anonymity and our deaf anger. A wafer is our shield, our gait is a lamentation, an agonized drift. We are young Acadians, we are without memory, marching in resignation to our supper in the fading light. Winter lasts forever, and we stumble blindly towards the hearth. The image of Durelle lying face down on the mat.

Someone found an address you could write to for a complete set of photographs of the Montreal Canadiens. You could also write to the Macdonald Tobacco Company to get a calendar, in colour, with all six teams in the National Hockey League. I carefully cut out the photos and stick them to the rough paper in my scrapbook. Above Saint-Simon, the vault of heaven is sprinkled with stars, the silence is unbreakable. Once in a while a whisper of wind brings hints of other destinations, snatches of other ideas, the murmur of rumours that other places exist, places we can never get to unless we strap on wings, like birds, and fly. Failing that, we drift and dream.

Aurèle Albert closes his book and spits onto the stove-top, a kingly gesture of propriety. Little droplets of his saliva dance on the hot metal surface. Tomorrow, there's a chance of freezing rain, and ice will probably coat the road into the village. We'll put on our skates and make like NHL stars, skate on the frozen bay to the end of the Earth. Saint-Simon will shrink behind us as new places come into view. We will skate and skate until our dying day, the date of which is tucked away in Aurèle Albert's black notebook. Perhaps on that day we'll finally understand the photos of Yvon Durelle on the thin pages of *L'Évangéline*, and of the winning Canadiens team on the calendar from the Macdonald Tobacco Company. And when we return to the frozen, durable ground, the world will shake itself awake and change from monochromatic grey to living colour, our red sweaters brilliant against the pale blue sky into which we will all rise with or without Aurèle Albert's predictions, each of which comes to nothing with the death of each one of us.

Gabriel Foulem brings his father's horse out onto the ice. The animal is unshod and cannot stand up. It sprawls on the ice, trying to get to its feet. It reminds me of the photograph of Yvon Durelle, the workhorse on his knees while Archie Moore struts about the ring, arms raised in triumph, apparently ready to ascend directly into heaven. Someone, a priest in a sermon, said that Christ had more courage than Durelle because he was not afraid to get up when he stumbled with the cross on the way to Calvary. But at least Durelle wasn't crucified. Surely that's a kind of victory?

We have to get a tractor to help the horse off the ice. Gabriel is definitely in for it. We watch the real, anticipated drama unfold under cover of stoic resignation. Most of us are of the opinion that life is an adventure, that we are at the mercy of the wind, that it is not for us to figure out directions and consequences.

Meanwhile, we walk, skates tied around our necks, throwing chunks of ice, making fantastic breakaways into Jacques Plante's net, easy, playful movements towards the only place we truly know: the place of winter warmth, of farewells to the long summer, a place where each of us counts on the cover of winter that is much too hard and always too long.

Twenty Minutes Above Montsouris Park

ROBERT SMITHSON died while trying to photograph his installation Amarillo Ramp from the air. He had been seized by a bizarre fascination with this work. A master of environmental art, he had once exhibited pebbles in triangular wooden boxes. In one of his articles, he talked about his fascination with rust, which he said was like life in its incessant need for transformation. In an earlier work, *Spiral Jetty*, he constructed a jetty in the shape a spiral by dumping truckloads of pebbles into a shallow lake. Of all the geometrical figures, he said, the spiral, like the line, is the only one that is still feminine in gender, even the circle having been masculinized by obscure associations that have nothing to do with it.

It had been a long meeting, one that seemed to go on forever. On page after page in her notepad, she drew spirals, all of
them spinning off into nowhere. She is trying to raise three children by herself, and sometimes when she got home she was so
angry she hurled increasingly unpredictable objects across the
room. They flew like heavenly bodies and smashed against the
walls, either sticking into the plaster or falling to the concrete
floor. One morning when she was late for work she excused
herself by saying she had had to go to the police station to get
her son, who'd spent the night there. The patience of women.
The anger of women. She snapped into telephones and drew
spirals, frustrated by the injustices of men and the incompre-
hensibility of modern life. *Modern Life. Modern Love.* Her lover
was younger than her and told everyone that she was the most
beautiful woman in the world, but he didn't know about the
spirals she traced so furiously when she needed to calm down,
or the way she threw herself with such abandon into unpredictable and unimportant tasks.

The clouds spiral above Montsouris Park. The camera is
mounted on its tripod, its glass eye ogling, constantly juxtapos-
ing the drift of puffy white forms against the deep blue back-

ground of the sky. Four maps complete a diagram showing the exact spot, down on the ground, where the monitor is set up. Another virtual reality recomposed in the confining space of the art gallery.

Wanting to bring the sky down to earth: an old idea. The spiral may be the way to do it, since at its base is another spiral that acts like a fractal, a portal through which we sink to the heart of things, to a place where nothing exists but wind, a place to which other heavenly bodies gravitate, worlds inhabited by people whose fate is unknown to us. I always wonder if this was the dimension Smithson entered when his plane spiralled into the earth, smashing into his own premeditated and premonitory installation.

Identities

MY VERY name is an identity crisis. The day I learned how to write it down I felt as though I had passed some kind of initiation test. By the time I had memorized all its twelve letters, put them in their proper order, learned which way the accents went, I had already learned how to write everything else.

I was born on April 7 but not baptized until the thirteenth. Apparently, with only a few hours to go before my baptism, my parents still hadn't come up with a name that suited me. With a stroke of genius, my brother suggested they check the saints calendar. It turned out to be the day of Saint Herménégilde, which was all they needed. I never learned if the decision had been unanimous or if there was one holdout in my family who had argued for a simpler name—Élide, perhaps, or Victor, or Alyre, or Existe or even Telex—something with fewer letters, one that slid more trippingly off the tongue, anything but this complicated, unique and bizarre appellation that sounds more like a title than a name.

The last snowstorm of the winter fell on April 7 that year, and my father, unable to get my mother to a hospital, had to fetch the village midwife, who hadn't brought a child into the world for years. There had been some hemorrhaging with my mother's previous pregnancy, and she had almost died at the age of thirty-seven. My father, Samuel (lucky him, only six letters) was forty-seven. All my life he played the role of the indulgent, well-wishing grandfather. His father, my real grandfather, was named Pholorome. I have always believed there is an affinity between our two names, which probably explains why I have always been interested in modernity and the necessity it generates in our lives!

Because of the terminal *e* in my name, people often think I am a woman, which is why my work has been included in an anthology of feminist writing and has swollen the ranks of an exhibition mounted by a curator desirous of making up for the absence of work by women in the secular canon. It could happen again at any time, since spelling errors are frequent, pronunciation difficult and curiosity unquenchable.

I could put together a collage of the numerous variations on my name that have come through the mail. Seeing my name misspelled on letters causes me the greatest angst. Not to be outdone, I once thought of restructuring the letters of my name to give it a more aristocratic appearance. By the subtle adjustment of capitals and spaces, for example, I could become Hermé né Gil de Chiasson.

Most of my friends call me Hermé, and it took me a while to resign myself to the fact that it is probably for the best. English people call me Herman, which at least is better than hearing my real name mangled or spending my life spelling it rather than saying it. In an article written against me, I was called Hermès Trismegistus, and I immediately wrote to the author, thanking him for calling me Three Times Master Hermès. At the time, I was writing broadsheets and working as a freelancer, like

Voltaire, who said, "I have never made but one prayer to God, a very short one: 'O Lord make my enemies ridiculous.' And God granted it."

There have been legal problems associated with my name. For example, there is the difficulty of squeezing my name into those little boxes that are provided on forms. When I simply have to write it down, my name often causes an ugly protuberance on the page. And if there is a list of names, mine, being so much longer than anyone else's, sticks so far out of the line it makes me feel self-conscious.

On the other hand, there is a certain comfort in knowing that I will never be mistaken for anyone else. The only famous Herménégilde I know of is Ermenegildo Zegna, the Italian designer. There is an Herménégilde Lavoie, one of the pioneers of Quebec cinema. Otherwise, I always jump up when I hear my name. In Quebec, near Sherbrooke, there is a village called Saint-Herménégilde, and I was so happy when I learned of it that I blew up a photocopy of the map so big that the letters practically disappeared into the texture of the paper.

Having a name that no one can pronounce often makes me the butt of jokes. That happened in Limoges, for example, a town in France to which I was once invited. Someone in the *Journal des francophonies en Limousin* wrote: "Despite having a name like a mouthful of marbles . . ." I was speechless. A name like a mouthful of marbles? I wanted to take the next plane home.

"My Name Is Herménégilde" is the title of a song that was popular for a while, and in the play based on Léandre Bergeron's *A Short History of Quebec*, one of the characters is called Herménégilde, to make it clear that he is not a man of the twenty-first or even of the twentieth century. I also remember hearing Fernand Seguin on the radio say that he had a neighbour named Herménégilde Hébert.

So there are some advantages to having this name. But there are also a few thorns. For one thing, it is hard to imagine a young Herménégilde. It is easier to think of me as an aged patriarch, which is the comment I get most frequently from people I meet who have only, until then, seen my name: there is such a disparity, they say, between my age and my name. Because of that I have often felt that my life is nothing but an attempt to live up to my name. Maybe someday I will finally be as old as I should be.

Photos of Morocco

ER FACE in partial shade behind a pair of red sunglasses, which I had painted white, at the wheel of a Renault 4 (yes, the one with the speedometer in the dashboard), speeding along a palm-lined road one winter in the 1970s, somewhere in Morocco, on Christmas vacation.

We'd driven through Spain. I'd photographed the windows of each hotel we slept in, the brutal light bursting into the darkened room, swallowing her shadow.

In the marketplace in Tetuán, I had my picture taken by a photographer who enlarged his negatives in a small structure that looked like a portable hovel. I photographed him while he worked, catching the withdrawn, shifty look in his eyes; he knew exactly how wide was the gulf of misery and misunderstanding that separated his world and mine, a gulf that nothing could ever bridge but these photographs.

In front of a hotel, a group of tourists was taking photos of a child on a camel. I went up and took some myself: boy on camel surrounded by cars. The child then got down off the camel and began collecting dinars, knowing that for a tourist to return from North Africa without photographs of camels and palm trees was tantamount to admitting that you were never really there. Exoticism doesn't come cheap.

In the Atlas Mountains, snow had begun to fall. There were warnings posted of the possibility of bandits, who would stop traffic by felling trees across the road and then robbing the immobilized travellers.

Photo of a tent flapping in the wind and a donkey eating blades of grass that stuck up through the snow. The melancholy of donkeys. It was late in the afternoon, the sun was falling rapidly over a dark world. The suggestion of solitude and of drifting through a world dessicated by dust and dryness. Wandering in circles the only way to cover this inaccessible land.

The smell of incense in the marketplaces at the end of the

day, the sweet odour mingling with the objects spread pathetically on the ground. At times they could be strangely moving, like that heap of cauliflowers on the square of red plastic, except that I had only black-and-white film in my camera and the red turned out black. I remember it as red; I'm fairly sure it was me who transformed it into black. Memory falters but photographs are forever, a modern version of "words fade but writing endures," and not bad as a publicity slogan. Any or all interested person or persons please take note.

Readings

I REMEMBER the day when I learned to read. I remember it exactly. The silence of summer, the odours exhaled by the fields, the flowers, the night, the sound of men talking in my family's general store, their arguments, their conversations, their violent, pointless dreams, their weariness, their waiting, their immobility, their movements in the darkness in the village lit by a single electric bulb over the front door of one of the lucky ones, the houses covered in grey shingles that folded into the darkness at night, the sense of being alone in the world.

The general store of my childhood seems like something out of a movie, with its striking colours, its wooden shelves painted yellow, its jukebox and its pool table. People went there to make unbelievable pronouncements, to engage in lengthy debates on highly improbable subjects. It was there I learned that a man's life was worth $3,500. For a long time, I wondered how anyone could come up with such a figure, the only possible explanation being the cost of the various materials of which the human body is composed, but even at that, materialistically speaking, even including the cost of construction, the amount seemed to me to be unlikely. It was hard enough to accept the idea that life could have a price at all, but it was even harder to believe that that price could be so precisely calculated.

One afternoon in winter, one of the customers grew indignant at the fact that they had spent so much money to put a man on the moon. Everyone knew that a creature from the moon had landed on Earth, had looked around and decided not to stay, and now here we were spending all that money to get him back to where he came from. The ensuing discussion ended in a series of shrugs. The customer was always right. Defeated by irony and cursing the lack of education forced upon him by those who profited from lying to him, he felt himself despised by those who, full of their own knowledge, placed themselves outside the lot of common mortals, a group to which he was so cruelly forced to belong.

I see my father playing billiards in his white shirt, grey hat, black suspenders. My mother and brother driven frantic by the accumulating bills, the credit given and never paid. Their thousand-and-one plans for escape.

It was in this picturesque setting that I stumbled upon the secret order of the alphabet, a code that until that moment had eluded me. I was in the store. I picked up an advertisement and began to read it, unaided. When my mother realized what I was doing she stopped and stared at me in astonishment, as though I had been born mute and had just spoken for the first time. I remember the sense of freedom, the towering vertigo that followed the event. I remember the day when I learned to read. I remember it exactly.

Video Game

THIS MAN turning on himself, having invented an ingenious game to set his internal clock, could it possibly be me?

To play this game, you need a clock, a video camera and a cassette. You place the cassette in the camera and videotape the clock. When the second hand sweeps across the twelve, begin turning with the camera in a circular motion. The idea is to circle around with the camera and return it to the clock again just as the second hand is back at the twelve, thus establishing a rotation that takes exactly one minute. If you can do this, you know that your biological clock is keeping perfect time.

Dan Graham has invented another video game that allows

you to psychoanalyze yourself, using a camera and a video monitor. First, you videotape yourself, telling the camera something extremely personal, something you've never told anyone before, something you've kept private for years. Then you place the cassette in the monitor and watch it, videotaping your own reaction to hearing your original declaration. Then place the second cassette in the monitor and tape your reaction to the first, and so on and so on until you lose interest, either in the game or your reactions to your reactions. By observing the decline in your responses to the original declaration, you chart a sort of alteration or disjunction between the sound of the original declaration and the image you are watching, between the present instant and the transformation of it that operates through time.

To me, the most fascinating use of video is the surveillance camera. People in subway stations, filing by in such a hurry, oblivious to the fact that they are being watched by the camera's intrusive eye; it does nothing but bear witness, which in the end becomes our sole reality.

According to most of us, video will not become an art form until it detaches itself from the wall, thus freeing itself from architecture to find its true home in the dull dumpsters we call art galleries and art museums, those final resting places for all defunct and unresponsive communication systems, stored under a diversity of names borrowed from the world of art—painting, printmaking, photography, cinema (which waits impatiently to be joined by its neonate sibling, video, the dying bleat of all systems on the road to eventual extinction). The only interesting question about video is, what will replace it? How else will we record with such exactitude, such ecstatic profusion, the gospels of a diffused age in which all experience is transformed and condensed into a signal as banal as it is ephemeral?

In the meantime, there is this turning, second-hand man, passing the time by foreseeing it, predicting the precise amount of it he is wasting, not only proving he is wasting it but recording his wasting of it as he wastes it. What better way to kill time, unless you prefer cursing and groaning? There goes the electronic sweep, hypnotizing an entire age, as precise and predictable as a time signal.

White as a Sheet

THIS MORNING a layer of light snow covers the yard in front of the house in which I have just slept as only a child can sleep. Everything is white. I gaze out at all this whiteness for hours on end. Overnight, the snow has clothed the world in its immaculate sheet. I want it to stay this way, no scratches or marks, no footprints marring the surface. A surface as flawless as a sheet of paper.

Perhaps this is the extension of another life, when I was Mallarmé or Edgar Allan Poe, but if so, I don't remember it. It's easy to step outside yourself this way. Poe's voyage to the North Pole, where, according to Ricardou, the page's blankness blending into the snow's whiteness constitutes one of the first instances of the Modern Novel.

People who come to the house put me in a bad mood because they ruin everything, they leave futile and illusory marks when they make themselves a path through the snow. When I tell my mother this, she tries to mollify my obsessiveness by telling me that there is no way to prevent such a desecration. People have to come and go. Sooner or later they have to make their marks. A door has to be either open or closed. Duchamp again, with his silence. He, too, must have loved snow.

I learn my lesson and take my medicine with as much patience as I am capable of. Maybe, without my being aware of it and in a completely painless way, I have at last learned the terrible law of creation and destruction that dwells in the artist like two of the faces of Shiva. The fact that we must destroy in order to create, that creation is a fire that must burn on the outside or else it will consume us on the inside.

I haven't had breakfast yet. I'm still watching the snow. Its amazing spectacle has become a revelation. This snow is questioning me. Hypnotizing me. Subconsciously, perhaps, I realize that the white surfaces are hiding something from me, something much greater and much more astonishing than I thought. I cannot resign myself to the idea that snow is nothing more than a weight upon the earth. I know that later there will be colours, words, stages or screens.

But for now, I listen. It's warm, a childhood warmth full of smells and odours, a warmth that excludes adults, who have already stopped noticing some things and are busy forgetting everything else. I am watching the snow, I have no wish to turn away from it, to turn indoors where I will go back to being blind. I am the keeper of the snow, of its whiteness, and I keep watch to see who will dare to break this moment and who, without knowing it, will put an end to this ecstatic vision.

Much later. I am in the Gaité-Montparnasse metro station, looking up the address of a shop that sells nothing but paper. Years have gone by, and I am once again what I always ought to have been. I go to this shop often. I spend hours in it, looking at sheets of paper, at their different textures, touching them. I never buy anything. Possession, I have learned, kills beauty. I believe it is better to leave beauty to its own fate and console myself with the fact that these objects exist, to be happy leaving them in their proper place, and to be alive and sharing their presence.

Just when I am about to give in to temptation, I rush out onto the sidewalk without making a purchase. This no doubt calls for an adjustment to my priorities, but I still prefer to draw on newsprint, even though I know that in the end my work will disintegrate, like confetti. Like snow. But what right do I have to inflict my doubts and errors onto a sheet of paper that is already, by virtue of its whiteness, a perfect work of art? I know what others would do in my place, probably on the very sheet that I was contemplating inside, but at least it won't be me who has to live with the weight of such pretension.

These papers are very dear to me. I don't want my work to derive its interest from the fact that it has been printed on expensive paper. And yet it must be so. I must move on without giving in too much to this obsession with the whiteness of yesteryear's snow. To see the world as a work, its surface as an illusion, a mask, a trick of the eye. I take up a piece of chalk, it doesn't matter which one, and I make a mark, it doesn't matter what. I have a vague idea of what is going to appear, of what must surge forth, but I take a stab at improvisation. Suddenly, the deception interferes with what I'm trying to do, and I see that I have to work with the surface rather than against it. Another dimension thrusts itself up through the paper, the canvas, the screen or the film.

A neighbour is walking with heavy steps across the field towards our house. There is something he needs to know. Without even being aware of the damage he is causing, he crosses the white yard, his footprints making craters and causing the earth to tremble at each step, his shadow falling on the snow like a hole in light. He advances, an unbeliever and an apostate, towards the porch and asks for some useless information as trivial and offensive as his presence, as unimportant as his words, as banal as his life. I vow to forget everything he has said. Nothing will remain of him except the memory of steam rising from his heavy woollen coat, his gaze as it sweeps across space, revealing his enormous transgression, the fragile claims of outraged beauty.

The work progresses, and I am so surprised by what it turns out to be that I forget what I had originally intended. I have buried the paper's pristine beauty under layers of signs and doubts and imprecations. The paper has disappeared, become something else. The snow has melted, opened up wounds through which I can see mud taking over the surface, expelling the whiteness. It's the end of autumn, or maybe the beginning of another spring. The man leaves. He is a salesman, unwelcome company. He limps. His horse is tired. He leads it by a leather strap, and it follows him through the village, giving off light like an aura. The man shouts angrily at it, their slow steps sceding the snow, in the gaze of a child who preserves the entire scene in his feverish, fragmentary memory.

Privileges

IT WAS A.H. who convinced L.H. that we absolutely had to have a hot press for mounting work that future generations might consider important enough to preserve. At the time, A.H. was working on his cow series: pastel pink and blue cut-out cows, like pop-up photographic figures, that no glue known to science would make adhere to the acid-free hardboard on which he was trying to mount them. But with his innate gift for diplomacy, his skill as a communicator and a firm eye on his own future status in the history of art, he had managed to convince L.H. that the press was a necessity none of us could live without. And his word was made flesh.

It was a time when the common run of mortals was busy

making plaster casts or inking zinc plates on which we had engraved etchings that we hoped would one day constitute our own frothy claims to greatness. A.H. had slightly outpaced the rest of us by having already quit his day job in order to concentrate on his sublimated visions of the world and its things. Everything in the viewfinder of his camera seemed clean, accessible and controllable. He appreciated the value of magic and was imbued with a quasi-divine mission, which he brought to the attention of L.H., who, as a war hero and great lover of Scotch whisky, was hoping for nothing more complicated than a little peace of mind and tranquility of soul.

We all know the kind of feelings that are stirred up in the human breast when it is confronted by a machine or a robot or any other type of toy that is destined to take over his world. If you recall the scene in Bertolucci's *1900*, in which the landowner demonstrates to his slack-jawed peasants the tractor with which he intends to replace them, you have a pretty good idea of the deplorably agitated emotions that gripped us at the sight of this new press, which opened our amazed eyes to the wonders of what until then had remained a distant modernity.

Before long, a whole herd of cows was resting comfortably

on A.H.'s acid-free boards. At first, he thought that the machine belonged to him and that he would be its proud and mythical guardian, but it soon became clear that we were all required to bow to the fetish of our new cult. T.W. was the first to lift the veil between us and the holy of holies, but then T.W. was second-in-command under A.H., the one in whom A.H. had placed his entire trust, his right-hand man, so to speak, the shadow of he who had walked in the valley of death. He was the first to experience the ecstasy of touching the warm metal, to let its warmth run up his hand and spread into his arm, then pass through his shoulder and into his head, which immediately began to swell. A.H., who was standing behind him, reassured him that the thing was supposed to produce that kind of reaction and that there was no need to make a fuss about it. All that was needed was faith. T.W. took his hand off the press and looked at A.H., his eyes glowing with gratitude for having thus been admitted into so closed and select a circle.

When it was my turn, it was so late and A.H. was so tired that there was no time for me to feel the effects that had transported T.W. to such Elysian heights, where the air is rarified and from whose bourn the traveller returns, blinded forever by the light and deafened by the sounds whose enticements render him terminally stunned. I didn't get along with A.H. all that well. I hated his cows, for one thing. I found them infantile, repetitive, Carolingian: in short, a kind of visual diarrhea. But in the name of freedom of expression, I refrained from making such disparaging comments, aware also of the fact that A.H. had his cabal and everyone regarded him as their wellspring of inspiration, Jesus crucified on a piece of hardboard. What could I say? God the Father Himself had parted the clouds to hand him the press, just as earlier, with His outstretched finger, He had created Adam from a lump of clay.

A.H. had thus become the Messenger, come down from the mountain with the sacred tablets under his arm. The problem was that I did not recognize him as such, and he, not to be outdone, no doubt found me too theoretical, too boastful, too full of my own modernist theories. A.H. despised theory. He had other goals, which had more and more to do with his status as the visual beast, which detracted somewhat from his image as the Messenger. That was only one of his many inconsistencies. Once the cows were marvellously and firmly hot-pressed to their hardboard field, still acid-free, A.H. took on a certain lassitudinous air. Perhaps he was dissociating himself from the party line so as not to run afoul of the Eternal Father. We'd see him wandering the halls of the school, looking for a new religion, flanked by a bevy of disciples curious as always to know what he had in his portfolio, which, although everyone knew that it contained nothing but hardboard, now nicely cowed, seemed to be as heavy as a set of stone tablets. With such an agenda, how could he be expected to find the time to share his solitude and know-how? Which he therefore kept for himself, convinced that if he lost himself in the expression of his own myth, he risked ending up an artisan on what seemed, from a distance, to be the periphery, the mere projection or mirage of what was once the core of its meaning. A.H. followed his path to glory; what he said was a hundred times more important than what he did. He had signed on for this course. One fine day he would light out for the big city, where fame would soon overtake and bury him in its ineffable rays.

As for L.H., who had blessed A.H. by procuring the instrument of his power, he retired content to have given back to the world what he had taken from it. T.W. disappeared into the setting sun, his cowboy hat transforming him into a shimmering silhouette of empty and gaping anonymity.

As for me, I'm just glad to have finally disburdened myself of the foregoing. I've been carrying it about with me for a while, and it was time I set it down. Those were memorable days, and there is no one left but me to record them.

Oscar de la Renta

IRST, AN intriguing full-page ad in the *New York Times*, a photograph showing a woman who seems to be looking over her shoulder to show us the cut of her clothing. Yes, she's a model. Behind her, a man in a doorway, smiling. We assume he is Oscar de la Renta, the couturier who must have designed the dress. The photo is slightly off-kilter, conveying the impression that the whole thing is unstable, a bit as though we are on a ship that is in the process of sinking. The photo, by Diane Arbus, a fashion photographer when she needed to put food on her table, is like a dream that captures the euphoria that reigned aboard the *Titanic*—we hear the frenetic sound of music as the ship slips under the icy waves.

This is followed by the obsessive clipping of this photograph, with lots of cropping to make dozens of versions that, arranged side by side, make a kind of cartoon. This print is then cut up again to make the images that are tipped into a book called *Oscar de la Renta and Other More or Less Related Stories*. (This all takes place in the United States, where no one has to be bilingual. Americans are kings: the world speaks whatever language they speak. It must save a lot of bother.)

Next to each image, on the left-hand page, is a found text. The idea is that, since we live in a society so saturated with images, there must be some link between them, and the text will explain the image. It's a never-never land in which we see so many strange and marvellous things. Nothing new about that, except that here the text is isolated, diminished before an image it cannot contain. This leaves the image free to roam about at random, even turn somersaults, as it seems to be doing. Thus, we see a woman's foot counterpoised against an ad for a miraculous prosthetic device that increases the size of a man's reproductive organ, a process to which humanity will surely not submit itself again. The image-text relationship is masculine-feminine: image (feminine), text (masculine). The idea could be enchanting, even fascinating, but succeeds only in being annoying and misleading. All that glitters.

From this problematic male-female relationship, meaning is born, and everything that comes after it. Poetry does nothing but recarve this dimension to infinity, proposing other routes, rewarding glamour and taming flashes of genius. Oscar de la Renta, his enigmatic smile, like a new *Mona Lisa* in a doorway in the *New York Times*. Who would have believed in such a metamorphosis?

Giotto

I DON'T REMEMBER what year it was. Another trip. Northern Italy this time. More places to check out, to inventory and catalogue, because we know that memory becomes saturated with impressions that deteriorate over time and so must be replenished with fresh stores of the mind's capital. Italy's cultural sector. In Florence, the usual round: the Baptistery, the Museum of Offices, the convent in which Fra Angelico painted his frescoes, or, should I say, his miracles. In Brescia, I met Achille Cavellini, an eccentric millionaire artist who had become a celebrity; he gave me an issue of *Playboy* in which his life story was printed on the naked bodies of two beautiful women. Two full bodies of work, such extravagance, what a harvest. But the real miracle that year took place in Padua.

It was cold that winter. I braked the car in a flood of historical light, the kind of light you see in great works of art, that makes you dream that you are really somewhere else, in another time, except you are aware that space has barely shifted. The guard opened the wrought-iron door, then a smaller door to the chapel, like a reliquary, containing the famous frescoes of Giotto, which he painted in the chapel at Arena. Coming face to face with beauty always brings me up short, temporarily blinds me. I'd seen these works before, in the Time-Life volume *The World of Giotto*, and I was worried that the originals would be disappointing. But they far exceeded anything I had expected. This was nothing like déjà vu, no romantic reincarnation in which I was recalling my former life as a court artist for some insane warrior-prince who commanded a monumental work for the future greater glory of himself or for the redemption of his faded pride.

No, what I experienced was more like what I'd felt in the cathedral at Chartres or in the abbey of Mont-Saint-Michel. The sudden sensation that a transient reality has taken temporary refuge in these stones, these colours, this light. The intense sharing of a belief that leaps across centuries. I stared at them for a long time, thinking that I didn't really believe in anything, not passionately in any case, not in anything that could motivate me to give my life to it. I live in an age of expectation, and, like everyone else, I endorse the gospels of cynicism and derision. What if I realized I had been wrong the whole time? How could I have made such a mistake? To wait, the sky menacing and deplorable over our heads, for the dessicated air to destroy everything in the fallout from a radio-controlled, classified, poisonous mushroom cloud.

By comparison, Giotto's sky suddenly seemed clear, free of constraint and fear. It made me believe in a heaven that promised something other than eternal damnation. It's not that I wanted to live in another era or to sing the praises of the good old times. I was content to remain in my own century. But I also wanted this sky above me, this spray of twinkling stars on the milky transept of the fresco, and these people around me in their solid, primitive poses, ethereal and corporeal, and these faded colours, honest as the crackling passage of time.

The fact is that Giotto did not paint to be part of a critical system or some "ism" but simply to express his place as the bearer of a common faith. He might have been doing something else as well, but I believe in that painting in the same way, I suppose, as in our contemporary obsession we believe in the 525—soon to be 3,000—lines on a video screen, or in the strident cries of the Internet or in Star Wars. Giotto exemplifies the doubts and the artifice of an era in painting, the most faithful communication system of his time. His was an act of faith that lasted at least as long as the electrons dancing about on our screens, leaving an empty, fragile sky behind the glow that passes through space and constitutes our own act of faith, coded in silicon chips and the latest claims of science.

Giotto, on commission, worked and innovated in a common language. People would come from great distances to devote long periods of time to viewing his paintings, to lose themselves in his vision of paradise. He painted great events like a reporter who, with his reassuring voice, signs on to bring us news of what he has witnessed: "Giotto here, speaking to you from the Mount of Olives. Behind me, slightly obscure because it's the middle of the night, you can just make out the figure of Christ.

He's the one on his knees, with his clothing spattered with the blood of his divine transpiration."

Cold permeates the stone. In the fields, the peasants gather firewood. Heavy tapestries keep the pervasive dampness out of the prince's chamber. The Tuscan countryside is filled with the sound of horses' footfalls, the slaughter on feast days; the smoke of incense parts to reveal the passion of his vision, like a stained glass window flooded with light, except that his is a brilliance that needs no external light; there is a luminosity in these robed figures, even in their surroundings, although the people are much more important than the space they move through. The intense blue, the honesty of his visual solutions, of his earthly paradise.

The Paleness of Things

SOMEONE HAD written in the gallery's visitors' book: "It's like childhood again, when you feel things in ways that are so new and so powerful that they stay with you for the rest of your life."

Dried flowers, heads sagging, petals stiff against the soiled veil that served as their backdrop, shards of broken glass poking through nylon bags, shreds of tissue paper sprinkled with red paint, but most of all the cut flowers in their delicate sarcophagi: that's what she would have seen and taken away in her eyes, later superimposing the show's fragility and transience on whatever else she saw, reinventing and, no doubt in the end, deforming them to produce her ever more exaggerated memories. She would go the distance.

In the winter, there was nothing to do but begin a work-in-progress of transient visions and moments, the distant glimmer of summer, its unforgettable and yet impossible to remember fragrances hovering just out of reach of the senses, the choking warmth of the heating system, the baseboard heaters, snow falling and her dancing behind the veil of illusions; nothing appealed to him in his woollen armour. But when she smiled with her naked hands in her angel's hair, he skidded on the ice to make her laugh. All that. Just then, at that precise moment in history, he conceived this poem, this monument, this fragile, moving mausoleum in which he would lie down beside her as in an ancient tomb from the time of queens and kings, when Death was trapped in leaded windows and the Devil was afoot on the land. Luckily, she protected him with her tender, red-gold smile, tracing with her finger the track of his errors, straightening despite herself the paths of his destiny so that he could invent more images for her, and his blood would never seep through the thin membrane of his heart and they would always see the same ocean. All that. She did it so well, especially when she showed him how she could melt winter wherever she went. But she did that in secret, her miracle to prove to believers that love existed.

One day he started to take some photographs. It was the last day; the next, he would unpin the roses and toss them into a cardboard box. The spell would vanish in a puff of smoke; she must be anonymous and secret. He had broken his promise to her. She made the images evaporate, disappear, dissolve within the camera itself, lost before they were developed, nothing left but the pale, blurred halo of her blonde hair against snow. Another variation on the theme that everything has its time, and then its time is over. Only memories are as eternal as rain.

Heresies

I knew these people, these two people, they
were in love with each other.

THUS BEGINS of one of the most moving monologues in the history of cinema. A man goes into a booth in a peep show and sees his wife, who, since she can't see him, asks him if he wants her to take off her sweater. It's the opening line for all lovers in a century in which everything is available and interchangeable. Every time I think of it I think of people I've known, of times when they were happy and a small part of their happiness rubbed off on me; they were in a state of grace that provides a foretaste of heaven, back when we had an inkling that heaven existed or that it was something worth waiting for.

Wim Wenders's *Paris, Texas* is based on the myth of Orpheus, the man who was told not to look back at his wife, but did, when he returned from the underworld. Lot's wife, who, when Sodom and Gomorrah went up in an atomic explosion, looked back and was transformed into a pillar of salt, not unlike certain victims of Hiroshima, petrified where they stood. The man-woman relationship, a perpetual war in which happiness is a negotiated ceasefire between battles. There is one long sequence in which nothing is said, but there the scene is laden with the weight of unspoken words, the desire to say one thing clearly once and for all, to confess for all time even if the confession itself, the simple act of enunciating it, is a form of derision. The thousand-year trajectory of a man who returns a child to his mother.

—Why didn't you keep him with you, Jane?

—I knew I would want to use him to fill up all the empty spaces in me.

Walking through a forest one afternoon in spring, he recalls a phrase that opens a whole book of memories. She is looking at the green of the forest with her green eyes, and for a moment he wonders which of them has stolen colour from the other. Walking beside a stream, he sees that across it someone is being buried while he has been rejuvenating in the mystery of her eyes. He had forgotten that one day he, too, would have to function in the world of fragmentation, in small moments miraculously untouched in the eye of the storm, a protecting silence, a luminous enigma.

That's when he sets out on the long march that will bring him to the underworld. He is condemned from then on to walk his entire life, to go wherever time pushes him, without rest or comfort, until he finds himself among those who, like him, had once lived on love's continent and had been exiled, over their dead bodies, to this remote island of grief.

The American Photograph
Since 1950

THE GLACIAL dampness ate at my heart. January, 1985, Paris. I was waiting to hear the disappointing verdict on my thesis on American photography. A few minutes before I was to begin my defence, my thesis advisor took me aside to tell me that my dissertation was riddled with errors; it was an old mania of mine, never taking a subject seriously enough to want to exhaust it.

I was renting a room at the Hotel Parc Montsouris, not far from the lake where I used to spend so many hours watching the ducks swim in front of a restaurant I never once went into.

The famous benches of the Sorbonne and the convulsive

anarchy of Paris crowds. In my mind's eye I saw her filigreed face, her eyes caked with makeup, her strange look crossing this strange room, her self-assurance, her electrifying words written on squared paper. Then we were in a car, driving full speed through the city, our precise, refined affirmations that made sense only in the intervals between heartbeats. My foreignness, her foreignness, and the letter *Z* that began her name like a flash of lightning, like a sword ripped through the night, her expression as fixed as the speed that was consuming us.

Paris, January, 1985. I am writing to you from the end of the Earth. I miss your laughter in the places we used to run to, where we forgot about the people who loved us and who worried at times that life could be so unfair. I can still hear the cries in the distance of that man lying on the ground who was being attacked and kicked. I had a split second, but the lighting wasn't good enough for a sharp image. I remember his cries, the shouted insults. I cannot repeat them here.

From the first, photography was an art of identification. But, as with all forms of expression, we began to believe that what it identified was reality. "Look. This is me." Things went downhill from there. As time passed, we found ways to make photography faster, to speed up the process. You could be captured in a photograph. "This is a photo of me. Did you see?" Soon the photograph was everywhere, wrapping the world in a thin film on which we reproduced ourselves in all sorts of distorted ways. "It's just a photo. It's not really me with those closed eyes, that open mouth, that head turned away. I would have looked completely different a millisecond later. I would have been sublime. I would have lived forever. Take it again, you'll see." That's what I had to say about the art of photography. A long, obsessive passage about identity and sign. That's all, folks. Thank you.

That afternoon we decided to make ourselves immortal, to prove we could be beautiful and good in the City of Light. We walked to the Palais de Chaillot, from which there was the most beautiful view of the Eiffel Tower. It was there that Hitler, in the small hours of his victorious morning in 1940, performed the little dance that many of us, including me, have seen in archival footage of the time, when he slapped the stones with his riding crop, overjoyed at the realization that Paris belonged to him, his performance preserved forever in the fragile annals of the twentieth century.

We have our own archives. The photo of us before the Trocadero fountain. There is a sort of jubilant triumph in our eyes, too, just from knowing that we had come so far. I was there. The photo as graffiti, as a way of removing all doubt. Proof positive.

They were all there. I had gone to see them. They had read my paper. I had seen their names on scholarly articles that I'd read to support my thesis, and now it was their turn to disapprove of the conclusions of my overlong text, my solitary exercise in writing whose eight hundred pages weighed my arm down to the ground. I had written the whole thing too quickly. They didn't point out my grammatical errors; they merely told me that I could have included more photocopies to illustrate my points. I thought of our laughter ringing off the stone walls and of the loneliness of being back in the places we deserted when we left to hawk our illusions somewhere else.

In my memory there remains this breakneck drive through Paris, her body pressed against mine, soaked in a futuristic fantasy we could never quite shake off. He was driving, commenting aloud on the state of our confusion, finding roundabout ways to tell me of his desire for her, of our common desire, in fact, of how he was pursuing this long and haunting trajectory towards her.

1985, Paris, January. The city is once again its sophisticated self: elegant, a bit nervous, a mass of memories, a tissue of lies. What is gone, most cruelly, is the sun's warm and luminous brightness on the boulevards, gone forever, gone for good, the bright green of the park melting into the choppy water of the lake, the sound of fountains cannonading into Sunday conversations, the melancholy of mornings after too much drinking, the minute time-lapse that separates us ever so slightly from feeling and laughter and singing, from indifference to the idea of wasting time, and from the indolence of living in a world of images that populate our indelible and yet so ephemeral archives.